The Blessings

of the

Beatitudes

Dennis J. Billy, C.Ss.R.

En Route Books and Media, LLC
Saint Louis, MO

⊛*ENROUTE*
Make the time

En Route Books and Media, LLC
5705 Rhodes Avenue
St. Louis, MO 63109

contact@enroutebooksandmedia.com

Cover Credit: Sebastian Mahfood from The Sermon of the Mount as depicted by Louis Comfort Tiffany in a stained glass window at Arlington Street Church in Boston. Photo by John Stephen Dwyer (March 2009). Wikimedia.org.

ISBN-13: 978-1-956715-75-0
LCCN: 2022943150

In loving memory of my father and mother

Michael Billy (1924-2009)
Lillian G. Billy (1927-1983)

Do not think that I have come to abolish the law or the prophets. I have come not to abolish but to fulfill. (Mt 5:17)

Acknowledgments

Parts of this book were previously published as: "*Humilitas*: Walking Humbly in an Unbelieving World," *Foundation Theology 2010: Faculty Essays for Ministry Professionals*, ed. John H. Morgan (Mishawaka, IN: Graduate Theological Foundation, 2010), 47-58 [Chapter Three]; "Blessed are the Single-Hearted: On Doing the One Thing Necessary," *Foundation Theology 2014* (Mishawaka, IN: Graduate Theological Foundation, 2014), 41-55 [Chapter Six]; "Truth and Peace of Heart," *Studia moralia, Supplemento* 3, 45(2007): 77-94 [Chapter Seven]. Except for those within direct quotations from the authors cited, all Scriptural citations come from *Holy Bible: New Revised Standard Version with Apocrypha* (New York/Oxford: Oxford University Press, 1989).

Table of Contents

Introduction

The beatitudes, some of the most beautiful words ever penned, are a blessing for all humanity. They point to a kingdom yet to come but already in our midst. They are not only poetic, but also upsetting and challenging. In his own day, Jesus had a reputation for turning on their heads the deepest assumptions of his listeners and exposing the deep-seated prejudices that masqueraded under the guise of religious piety. He challenged his listeners to look beyond the narrow confines of their limited belief systems to get a glimpse of the compassionate love of "Abba, Father." One does not have to go far in the Gospels to find Jesus giving a teaching or telling a parable that moves the ground from under the feet of his listeners and invites them to look with new eyes at the world around them. The beatitudes open Jesus' "Sermon on the Mount" in the Gospel of Matthew 5:3-10 and, taken together, are one such instance where he helps us to see what the kingdom of God is like.

St. Augustine of Hippo (354-430), one of Christianity's preeminent theologians, has a unique approach to the beatitudes. As Servais Pinckaers points out, soon after his ordination in 391, Augustine was entrusted by his bishop with the ministry of preaching in Hippo. After a few months preparing for this arduous task, he came out with a commentary on the Sermon on the Mount, which he saw as a veritable "charter for Christian living" and the beatitudes themselves as both a hermeneutical key for interpreting the whole sermon and providing an outline of the various stages of the Christian life. What is more, he aligned the first seven beatitudes with seven gifts of the Holy Spirit and the seven petitions of the Our Father.[1] The eighth beatitude, he claimed, embraced all that came before it and represented the fullness of Christian life that "diminishes our rebellion against the injustice done to us because of Christ and gives us the strength and joy to suf-

---

[1] See Augustine of Hippo, *On the Sermon on the Mount*, Bk I, chaps. 1-5; Bk 2, chap. 11; Servais Pinckaers, *The Sources of Christian Ethics*, trans. Sr. Mary Thomas Noble, O.P. (Washington, D.C.: The Catholic University of America Press, 1995), 141-63.

fer for him."[2] Out of respect for this venerable father of the Church, I will follow Augustine's enumeration of seven beatitudes and look to the eight as a recapitulation and culminating point of the previous seven.

This book is about the vision Jesus sets before his hearers of a world ruled by justice and love. The beatitudes challenge the accepted religious sentiments of the day. They single out the poor as God's favored ones. They pronounce blessings over the downtrodden and outcasts of society, the very ones who were judged unclean by the Law and were thought to be tainted by sin. They present a vision of a world where those who have not reap the benefits of God's benevolent gaze. They proclaim a kingdom in which the commonly accepted standards of the world have given way to an entirely new system of values. They affirm God's compassionate love for the poor and unfortunate and repudiate all that perpetuates the

---

[2] Servais Pinckaers, *The Spirituality of Martyrdom...to the Limits of Love*, trans. Patrick M. Clark and Annie Hounsokou (Washington, D.C.: The Catholic University of America Press, 2016), 27.

seemingly unending spiral of hatred and preju-
dice.

The beatitudes represent a vision of a world
where the weak and the lowly matter and where
the poor and the hungry are fed. Jesus does much
more, however, than merely present an attractive
vision of a kingdom yet-to-come. He promises his
hearers that it will not only one day come to pass,
but that it has already begun to take shape in their
very midst! The blessing of the beatitudes is the
hope that rises within all who listen to and follow
the call of the kingdom in their hearts. Without
that hope, there would be no place in the human
heart for the Spirit of God to dwell, and the kingdom of God would not be able to reach its com-
pletion. With that hope, all things are possible—
even the unspoken miracle that turns a hateful
heart into a tranquil reservoir of divine peace.

Chapter One

Blessed are the Poor in Spirit

"Blessed are the poor in spirit, for theirs is the kingdom of heaven" (Mt 5:3). Love of God and neighbor make up the very core of Jesus' teaching and beautifully illustrates the meaning of the first beatitude. In his book, *With Open Hands,* Henri J. M. Nouwen describes growth in the spiritual life as a movement from clenched fists to open hands.[1] Clenched fists symbolize those self-centered people who go through life clinging to power, possessions, and pleasure: anything that will make them stand out and satisfy their needs. Open hands, by way of contrast, symbolize those who center their lives on others and find fulfillment by placing the needs of others before their own. Jesus is a perfect example of someone who lived his life with open hands. He centered his life on fulfilling the will of his Father in heaven by serving those around him.

---

[1] Henri J. M. Nouwen, *With Open Hands* (Notre Dame, IN: Ave Maria Press, 1972), 12-22.

Poverty of Spirit

To be poor in spirit means that we are not going through life trying to squeeze everything we can out of it to satisfy our own selfish needs and desires. Rather than trying to wrest as much out of life for our own benefit, we look at those around us and try to meet their needs. Rather than clinging to externals and defining ourselves by them, we loosen our grip and do not allow them to become the measure of our self-worth. Poverty of spirit involves putting all things, even good things, in their proper perspective. Rather than making an idol out of created goods and all that flows from them, we see them in relationship to the source from which they came and thank God for having given them to us.

When seen in this light, poverty of spirit refers not to a particular lack of spirit in us, but to a spirit entirely focused of God and thus able to view all other things in their proper light. The kingdom of heaven belongs to those who are poor in spirit, because they understand that their ultimate good rests in God alone and that all else pales in comparison. When material goods become secondary, their true worth shines forth. Rather than being worshipped as idols by those who place the ultimate meaning of their existence in them, they become subordinate goods to be used for the building of God's kingdom. Their relative worth in relationship to God enables the poor in spirit to loosen their grip on them and be generous in the way they use them. A person who approaches life with open hands does not cling to the goods of this world and is even willing to let go of them when the need arises. The poor in spirit understand that all good things come from the hand of God and, for this very reason, are to be shared with others. They believe everything they possess—wealth, reputation, position, and the like—comes from God and ultimately will return to God. Rather than clinging to these things, they receive them humbly, hold them gently, and offer them freely.

The early Christians prayed with open hands raised heavenward to God. This *orans* posture beautifully expresses the spirit of the first beatitude. With their hands lifted to God, those pray-

ing in this manner expressed an inner attitude of
humility and openness to God. By extending their
arms skyward, they were telling God that he was
their deepest treasure and that they wished to
cling to him alone and not to the things of this
world. Lifting their arms to God in this way also
indicated a desire for a deep, intimate relationship
with God. They loved God so much—with all
their heart, mind, soul, and strength—that they
wanted to put their arms around him and hold
him as a child would hold on to a parent. To live
life with open hands means trusting in God's fa-
therly care in all times, places, and circumstances.
It lies at the very heart of what it means to be his
adopted sons and daughters. To be poor in spirit
is to see oneself as a child of God who depends on
him for everything. This utter dependence on God
is the gateway to holiness and lies at the very heart
of spiritual childhood.

Becoming Poor in Spirit

   In our spiritual journey, most of us are caught
somewhere in the middle, between clenched fists

and open hands. Although we are likely not entirely closed in on ourselves, we are also aware that we have a long way to go if we wish to live as Jesus lived. The real question before us is whether our hands are closing or opening, becoming clenched fists, or opening to others. If we are in the process of closing our hands and turning them into fists, then we are selfishly turning inward and closing ourselves off to the movement of the Spirit in our lives. If, however, we are gradually opening them up in service to others, then we are slowly becoming more Christ-like in our thoughts, words, and actions. Poverty of spirit involves taking the latter route. It means that we recognize our need to let go of ourselves so that we can let God shape us according to his providential plan for us.

To be poor in spirit does not necessarily mean that we fully understand and embody a life lived with open hands. Rather, it indicates awareness on our part of the goal toward which we are tending and a desire to do all we can to reflect in our lives the values it represents. When coupled with a trusting assurance that Jesus' presence in our lives will eventually carry us there, this humble recognition reveals our own sense of the fragility of our human situation and our need for God in everything we do. It indicates a deep knowledge of our own limitations and a desire to always depend on the Lord. It acknowledges God's sovereignty over all creation and looks to him alone as the source of all good things.

Jesus blesses those who are poor in spirit because they recognize their proper place in the order of creation and rely on their Creator (rather than themselves) for the inspiration and guidance they need to live holy and grace-filled lives. Because he always meets us where we are and brings us a little farther along the way, we can surmise that poverty of spirit has a wide range of possible embodiments. Some people may be more "poor in spirit" than others because they have abandoned themselves completely to the present moment and have come to depend more and more on the Lord in their daily activities. What matters most is not where we are along this spectrum, but whether we are committed to the process of approaching life with open hands. The key to understanding "poverty of spirit," in other words, is whether our hands, wherever they may be along the range of possibilities, are moving inward or outward, whether they are turning into clenched fists or moving outward toward open hands. The poor in spirit are those who have committed themselves to the process of opening their hands (and their hearts) to God, their Creator.

Blessed Are the Poor in Spirit

The words of the first beatitude also emphasize the communal aspect of poverty of spirit. Jesus says, "Blessed *are* the poor in spirit, for *theirs* is the kingdom of heaven." The wording indicates that we do not come to depend on God solely through our own personal relationship with God (as important as that may be), but through our relationships with him and others. God, in other words, relates to us first as a people and only secondarily as individuals. If the Jews are God's chosen people, Christians have been chosen by God to belong to a New Israel and are members of Christ's mystical body. The beatitudes in general (and the first in particular) are a communal gift and exist in us only because Christ has given them to us. Because of his total dependence on the Father, Jesus embodies poverty of spirit to the utmost degree. We can become poor in spirit only to the extent that we share in his divinized humanity through life in the Spirit.

Poverty of spirit, Jesus maintains, leads to the kingdom of heaven. The poor in spirit are blessed because of their trust in God's providential hand in their lives. Because they reach out to him with open hands, God reaches down and extends his open hands in friendship to them. Jesus once said, "No one has greater love than this, to lay down one's life for one's friends. You are my friends if you do what I command you. I do not call you servants any longer, because the servant does not know what the master is doing; but I have called you friends, because I have made known to you everything I have heard from my Father" (Jn 15:13-15). Jesus has laid down his life for us and now calls us his friends. Because he is one with the Father, he reveals to his friends everything the Father has revealed to him. Because he is in the Father and the Father in him (Jn 14:10), our friendship with Christ gives us a privileged knowledge of the Father.

The poor in spirit share in Jesus' poverty of spirit and, in doing so, have gained access to the kingdom of heaven. Everything in this kingdom has to do with the friendship with God. There are three marks of friendship: (1) benevolence, or actively seeking another's well-being, (2) reciprocity, in that the relationship must be mutual, and (3) a mutual indwelling, in the sense that each person carries the other within his or her heart.[2] The early saints were known as the "friends of God."[3] Because of Jesus' total dependence on the Father, and because of our total dependence on Jesus, we too have the capacity for holiness; we to can become saints, that is, close, intimate friends of the Father. The poor in spirit are blessed because they share in the joy and happiness of God's intimate

---

[2] See Paul Waddell, *Friendship and the Moral Life* (Notre Dame, IN: University of Notre Dame Press, 1989), 130-41.

[3] See Peter Brown, *The Making of Late Antiquity* (Cambridge. MA: Harvard University Press, 1978), 54-80.

love. The Holy Spirit, the intimate bond of love between the Father and the Son, now dwells in our hearts. In the words of St. Alphonsus de Liguori, "the paradise of God...is the heart of man."[4] The poor in spirit thus have to capacity to become living tabernacles of God. Because of their friendship with Jesus, and the mutual indwelling he shares with the Father, they can now become temples of the Holy Spirit. The poor in spirit are blessed, because they are joyful, happy, holy, and share in the intimate love of the Triune God.

Rich in God's Spirit

The poor in spirit seek to empty themselves of undue attachments to all created things so that they can be filled the Spirit and be able to respond to his quiet promptings. They are poor in spirit to become rich in the Holy Spirit. This process of self-denial is a sign of authentic discipleship since

---

[4] Alphonsus de Liguori, *The Way to Converse Always and Familiarly with God* in *The Complete Works of Alphonsus de Liguori*, ed. Eugene Grimm (New York: Redemptorist Fathers, 1886-94; reprint ed. 1926-27), 2:395.

it reflects the kenotic self-emptying of Christ in the mystery of the Incarnation. Led by the Spirit of Christ, the poor in spirit are empowered to respond to Jesus' call to discipleship: "If any want to become my followers, let them deny themselves and take up their cross and follow me" (Mk 8:34).

Following Christ means going where he has gone and where he is going. Just as Jesus entered our world in the mystery of the Incarnation, gave himself to us completely to the point of dying for us in the mystery of his passion and death, became nourishment for us in the mystery of the Eucharist, and a source of hope for us in the mystery of his resurrection and ascension into heaven, so must we, his disciples, enter the worlds of those around us, give ourselves completely to others, perhaps even to the pint of dying for them, become a source of nourishment for them, and a source of hope. As Jesus' disciples, we follow him by making his narrative our own so that, as members of his mystical body, we might bring Christ to others in the concrete circumstances of daily life.

The poor in spirit possess the kingdom of heaven because they know the difference between what does and does not matter. They are like the man who, having found a treasure hidden in a field, goes and sells all he owns to buy the field (Mt 13:44). Or, again, they are like the merchant in search of fine pearls who, having found one of enormous value, went and sold all he possessed to buy it (Mt 13:45). The poor in spirit live for God and God alone. All else is secondary. We are aware of our own spiritual poverty and know that only God can satisfy our deepest longings and desires. We seek to empty ourselves of all undue attachments to the things of this world to be befriended by God and filled with his Spirit. For us, friendship with God is the pearl of great price, the indwelling of the Holy Spirit, the hidden treasure found buried deep in the soil of our souls.

With Open Hands

The poor in spirit wish to go through life with open hands. They hold on to nothing and seek nothing but the open hand of God. God has extended his hand to humanity in the person of Jesus Christ, who entered his creation to redeem and sanctify it. This open hand is ultimately one of friendship. Those wishing to clasp it must let go of everything and allow God to pull them out from their sinful misery so he can lift them to heights beyond their wildest dreams. "God became human so that humanity might become divine," St. Athanasius of Alexandria tells us.[5] By befriending us, God elevates us by allowing us to share in the intimacy of his divine love. To be a friend of God is to be numbered among the saints. Poverty of spirit is essential for holiness. As St. Alphonsus de Liguori reminds us, "The light of the sun cannot enter a crystal vessel filled with earth; in a heart occupied with attachments to pleasures, wealth, and honors, the divine light cannot shine."[6]

How does one become poor in spirit? Once again, the image of the open hands comes to mind. As pointed out earlier, most of us are in the process of either closing our hands or opening

---

[5] Athanasius of Alexandria, *On the Incarnation*, 54.3.

[6] Alphonsus de Liguori, *The True Spouse of Jesus Christ* in *The Complete Works of Alphonsus de Liguori*, 10-11:489.

them. Our hands are neither fully opened nor fully closed. To be even more precise, most of us are in a constant state of flux: one moment our hands are opening and the next moment, they are closing. We identify strongly with the words of the Apostle Paul, "I do not understand my own actions. For I do not do what I want, but I do the very thing I hate" (Rom 7:15). Given this stark reality, what can we do to ensure that our hands are moving in the right direction? What can we do to make sure that we are going through life with open hands? What is the secret of the first beatitude? How can we become or at least enter the process of becoming poor in spirit?

The answer, quite simply, is prayer. St. Alphonsus de Liguori, called prayer "the great means of salvation."[7] He taught that everyone received sufficient grace to pray and that mental prayer (what today we often call, "meditation") was morally necessary for salvation, meaning that

---

[7] Alphonsus de Liguori, *Prayer, The Great Means of Obtaining Salvation and All the Graces Which We Desire of God* in *The Complete Works of Alphonsus de Liguori*, 3:13.

it would be very difficult for us to find our way to God without it. One of his most important sayings regarding prayer is quoted in the *Catechism of the Catholic Church*, "Those who pray are certainly saved; those who do not pray are certainly damned."[8] To put it less bluntly, if we pray, we will eventually find out way to God and experience the fullness of life. If we do not, we will lose our way (both in life and after life) and wind-up spending eternity trying to fill a giant hole in the depths of our souls with all sorts of created things that do not satisfy because only God can fill it. The poor in spirit are, first and foremost, men and women of prayer. They know that God alone can save them, and that prayer alone is the only way in which they can remain friends with God.

Prayer is nothing but "the raising of one's heart and mind to God or the requesting of good things from God."[9] Our prayers can be spoken as in *oratio*, or vocal prayer (as when we recite the

---

[8] Ibid., 3:49. See also *Catechism of the Catholic Church,* Vatican City: Libreria Editrice Vaticana, 1994), no. 2744.

Our Father or the Hail Mary). They can be mental, as in *meditatio,* or meditation (as when we talk
to God quietly in our minds). They can even be
wordless, as in *contemplatio*, or contemplation (as
when we rest quietly and wordlessly before the
tabernacle). They can also be communal, done
together in families, and prayer groups and especially in *liturgia* (as when we gather as God's people to celebrate the sacraments).[10]

Each of these types of prayer—*oratio, meditatio, contemplatio, liturgia*—corresponds to the
physical, emotional/intellectual, spiritual, and
communal dimensions of our human makeup,
which are echoed in the Apostle Paul's emphasis
on the tripartite anthropology of body, soul, and
spirit (see 1 Th 5:23), as well as the corporate dimension of our being members of Christ's body
(see 1 Cor 12:12). In a special way, all these elements come together when we gather for Eucharist. We express ourselves physically to God

---

[9] John Damascene, *On the Orthodox Faith, 3:24.*
Cited in *Catechism of the Catholic Church,* no. 2559.

[10] *Catechism of the Catholic Church,* nos. 1071-73,
2700-24.

through vocal prayers, songs, gestures, and engaging the senses with art, music, incense, colorful vestments, and the like. Our minds are nourished through the proclamation of God's Word and the homilies we hear that seek to instruct our minds and hearts. Our spirits, moreover, are nourished at the pregnant moments of silence, perhaps after the homily or after Communion, when we rest in God's presence in our midst and in our hearts. And we do this together, as God's people, a community of believers gathered out of love for God and a desire to serve him by living for him.[11]

Since each relationship with God is unique, it follows that each of our prayer lives will also be distinct. The key to prayer for us is to find an appropriate rhythm that incorporates each of these dimensions in a way that best enables each of us, as individuals, to give glory and honor to God. It is also important for us to ask ourselves which form of prayer we rely on the most and which we overlook and need to develop. For Irenaeus of Ly-

---

[11] Dennis J. Billy, *Evangelical Kernels: A Theological Spirituality of the Religious Life* (Staten Island, NY: Alba House, 1993), 170-78.

ons, "The glory of God is man fully alive!"[12] We become fully alive when each of these dimensions of our human makeup is given to God in prayer in a way that resonates deeply with (and in sync with) our own unique personalities. Our prayer to God should issue forth from the depths of our beings and embrace every aspect of who we are: the physical, emotional, intellectual, spiritual, and the social. Each of us is like a facet of a diamond that reflects the light of God's glory in a way that no one can replicate. Our prayer polishes God's image in us so that it can reflect the light of divine grace in a way that is distinct and unique in the world. The poor in spirit take to heart the words of the Apostle Paul: "Rejoice always, pray without ceasing, give thanks in all circumstances; for this is the will of God in Christ Jesus for you" (1 Th 5:16-18). Prayer, for them, is the spiritual air that they must breathe in and out, night and day, to empty themselves and remain in close, intimate friendship with God.

---

[12] Irenaeus of Lyon, *Against the Heresies*, 4.20.7.

Conclusion

The first of Jesus' beatitudes lays the groundwork for all that follows. Without poverty of spirit, we cannot focus on God, because we have to many distractions and are not empty enough to allow the spirit to inhabit our hearts and do his work in us. As a result, the other beatitudes fail to take root and flourish. Rather than being holy and happy, we give in to the ever-present downward pull of life that ultimately ends in sadness, misery, and death. The kingdom of heaven belongs to the poor in spirit because they place their entire trust in God and understand that he alone can lift them out of their misery and bless them with the riches of the life to come. For this reason, the poor in spirit are those who live in constant hope of one day seeing God face-to-face and thereby experiencing the fullness of life.

It is important to note that poverty of spirit is more a process that a fait accompli. The reason why is clear. In our earthly sojourn, a gap will always exist between where God wants us to be and where we are. The important question we need to ask ourselves each day is whether that gap is getting larger or smaller. A life dedicated to constant prayer will narrow the gap between vision and reality, between the ideal and the real, to the point that it will gradually disappear or become so small that it will be negligible. If those who pray will one day become completely poor in spirit, those who do not will spend eternity wallowing in the shadow of the clenched fist.

As the image of open hands suggests, the key factor is whether our hands are opening or closing. Even if we ourselves experience a constant moving back and forth in this process (with our hands opening a little, then closing a little, then opening a little again, and so on), the overall movement of our hands will tend toward the direction of openness, so long as we remember that it is the power of the Spirit at work in our lives that accomplishes the feat. The poor in spirit, in other words, recognize their limitations and allow God to enter their hearts and take over. Their poverty of spirit enables them to become rich in the Spirit—and that makes all the difference.

The Blessings of the Beatitudes

- What is your understanding of poverty of spirit?
- Do you agree that it has to do with our letting go of undue attachments?
- Have you ever experienced poverty of spirit in your life?
- What prevents it from happening?
- What promotes it?
- Do you consider yourself to be poor in spirit?

Prayer

Lord, help me to be poor in spirit. Enable me to experience it in my heart and in my relations with, family and friends, my community, and in society at large. Help me to let go of all that gets in the way of my relationship with you. Help me, Lord. Help me! I want to follow in your footsteps and be poor in spirit like you.

Chapter Two

Blessed are those who Mourn

"Blessed are those who mourn, for they will be comforted" (Mt 5:4). In the second beatitude, Jesus tells his listeners that sorrow will one day give way to joy, that grief will turn to gladness, that every heartbreak will be healed, and every lament transformed. C. S. Lewis tells us that mourning is not a state but a process.[1] When we lose a loved one, someone very close to us, we first find it difficult to accept and shake our heads in disbelief. In time, the harsh reality of death overtakes us, and our hearts are numbed by what has happened both to us and to our loved ones. Then the pain sets in. The loss of a loved one is very much like an amputation.[2] We feel as though we have lost a part of our own selves. The wound goes deep, deep into the marrow of our bones and the deepest recesses of our hearts. A part of us has died

---

[1] C. S. Lewis, *A Grief Observed* (New York: Seabury Press, 1963), 68.

[2] Ibid., 71.

along with our beloved, and we know instinctively that life will never be the same. With the passage of time, the grief may wane but will never fully go away. Our faith gives us hope that we will one day be reunited with our loved one, and we long for that day as watchmen wait for the coming of the dawn.

Mother of Sorrows

Mary of Nazareth, the mother of Our Lord, mourned the death of her Son long before she knelt at the foot of the cross from which he hung and suffered his last agonizing moments of earthly life. Years before, soon after her son's birth, she was told by the prophet, Simeon, when she and Joseph presented him in the temple, that a sword would pierce her heart, that he would be a sign of contradiction, and that through him the thoughts of many would be revealed (Lk 2: 34-35). One of her many titles is "Our Lady of Sorrows" and tradition tells us that seven touched her in a profound way: the prophecy of Simeon, the flight to Egypt, the loss of the child Jesus, meeting Jesus along the *Via Dolorosa*, the crucifixion of Jesus, holding him in her arms when he is taken down from the cross, and his burial soon afterwards. She is sometimes depicted in Christian art with seven swords piercing her heart. If there was anyone who knew what it was like to grieve over the loss of a loved one, it was Mary, the mother of Our Lord. Jesus himself must have been aware that his mother's suffering was intimately and intensely tied to his, and one wonders if he had her in mind when he uttered the words of this second beatitude.

Mary's mourning, as we now know, eventually turned to great joy. She was comforted by her Son when she met him after his Resurrection and by the descent of his Spirit and birth of the Church in the upper room on Pentecost (Acts 1:14). Our Lady of Sorrows is also known as "Comforter of the Afflicted." Just as Jesus gave his mother to the beloved disciple as he hung from the cross (Jn 19:26-27), so too does he give her to us to comfort us in all our sorrows and afflictions. What is more, just as mourning is a process, so too is comforting. To comfort someone means to accompany them in their grieving, listening to them, making time for them, journeying with them in the absence of their loved ones. Like her Son, Mary always meets us where we are and helps us take the next small step toward healing, holiness, and wholeness. She does so by simply being herself and by being to us what she was (and is) to Jesus—a Mother! Mary, Mother of the Church, brings a sense of warmth and belonging to the community of believers. She knows our needs—physical, psychological, intellectual, spiritual, social— and does her best to provide for them. She intercedes for us with her son and wants nothing more than to draw us closer to him. She sees her Son in us because we are members of his Mystical Body. Mary comforted her Son throughout his earthly life and promises to do the same for us.

Mary's fiat, "May it be done to me according to your word" (Lk 1:38), points to the close union of her will with God's will. The two are so closely intertwined that it would be difficult to distinguish one from the other. Her sole desire in life is to fulfill God's will in her life and in ours. She does so by watching over us with motherly care, interceding for us before her son, and actively seeking our well-being. In our times of grief and mourning, she comforts us by reminding us of her own sorrows and pointing to the life of her gloriously resurrected Son. She promises us that, as happened in her own life, our own sorrows will be transformed into joy. She who conceived by the Holy Spirit tells us that the fruit of her womb came into this world to conquer death by uniting his divinity to our humanity and entering our world with all its trials and tribulations, so that we might enter his.

Comforting the Sorrowful

Science tells us that there is a twofold catabolic and anabolic movement in nature. There are processes that break down living matter into simpler, less complex substances, and others whereby the reverse happens. Matter is continuously being decomposed and its remains transformed into living organisms. The fall foliage becomes compost, which, in turn, becomes food for plants, which in turn become food for livestock, which in turn be-

come food for human beings. There is, in other
words, an inescapable downward and upward
movement written into the very fabric of our existence.

Our mourning takes place against the back-
drop of this twofold dynamic of life and death.
Much of it, if not all, stems from our experience of
the catabolic, downward movement. The "tears of
things" (*lacrimae rerum*), the poet Virgil tells us,
are woven into the warp and woof of our earthly
lives.[3] "What goes up must come down," the ad-
age goes. We who are born are also doomed to
die. We mourn every time we experience this
downward pull of nature, especially when we suffer the loss of a loved one. Hearts are broken and
tears shed not only because we mourn the deaths
of those we love, but also because we sense the in-
evitability of our own deaths looming in the back-
ground.

The second beatitude reflects this same twofold movement that has found its way into the
fabric of our daily lives. Mourning the loss of a
loved one corresponds to the downward, catabolic

---

[3] Virgil, *Aeneid*, 1.462.

pull that leads to decomposition and decay. We mourn the deaths of our friends and loved ones because their passing from this life reminds us that we all are dust and one day shall return to it. Since we often live our lives in a state of denial (or at least are only peripherally aware) of this sobering truth, the death of someone close brings us face to face with this harsh reality and reminds us that it is not something we can simply ignore or hide from. Comforting those who mourn, by way of contrast, corresponds to the upward, anabolic movement that leads to new life and higher levels of existence. By promising us that those who mourn will be comforted, Jesus is reminding us that we are more than dust, that life continues after death, and that a new, transformed existence awaits us.

"God became man so that man might become divine." As we saw in the last chapter, this simple statement from one of the Church fathers reminds us that, when all is said and done, Jesus himself is the comfort of those who mourn. To heal and ultimately transform our wounded nature, God entered our world (in the mystery of the Incarnation), gave himself to us completely (in the mystery of his passion and death), became a nourishment for us (in the mystery of the Eucharist), and a source of hope (in the mysteries of his resurrection and ascension into heaven).[4] This fourfold Christological movement reflects the twofold upward and downward, anabolic/catabolic movement enmeshed in human existence. The kenotic, self-emptying mysteries of the Incarnation and Jesus' passion and death correspond to the downward, catabolic pull the leads to death, while the divinizing, transforming mysteries of the resurrection and ascension correspond to the upward, anabolic pull that rises to new life. Lying at the very center of Jesus' redemptive mysteries, the Eucharist immerses us in both the upward and downward movements of life. Because it immerses us in the mystery of his sacrificial death on Calvary, it corresponds to the downward, catabolic movement toward decay and decomposition. Because it brings into our midst the body and blood of our risen and glorified Lord, it reflects the upward, anabolic thrust toward higher levels of existence.

---

[4] Billy, *Evangelical Kernels*, 19-28.

When we eat of his body and drink of his blood, both processes are present. When we eat and drink of the flesh and blood of the Son of Man, we both digest and are digested. We take Jesus into ourselves and he, in turn, takes us into himself. Jesus, you might say, is our comfort food—and we, his.

As followers of Christ, we too are called to comfort those who are mourning the loss of their friends and loved ones. We do so by doing what Jesus did (and, of course, always with his help). We enter the lives of those who mourn by meeting them where they are. We give ourselves to them completely by accompanying them in their mourning and listening to them. We nourish them by wiping away their tears and providing spiritual and bodily sustenance for them. We become a source of hope for them by reminding them through our quiet, loving presence, that love is stronger than death and that Jesus himself has conquered death by embracing its deadly sting and overcoming it. Jesus acts in the world today through the members of his body, the Church. One of the ways he comforts those who mourn is by inspiring his faithful followers to allow him to live through them so he can touch the sorrowful and grieving hearts in the world today, wipe away their tears, and encourage them to live in hope.

The Mo(u)rning of 9/11

Probably one of the most harrowing times in recent history that brought much of the world together (if not all) were the terrorist attacks on the World Trade Center on September 11, 2001. This tragedy initiated a sense of compassion that reverberated throughout the entire world. This was terrorism on a large scale. The perpetrators of the crime, members of al Qaeda and those affiliated with them, resorted to very devious and nefarious means to take the lives of almost 3,000 people of many nationalities. What occurred was not a sin against the United States of America, but against all humanity. Violence in the name of religion cannot be tolerated in any shape or form. The action of these terrorists reminds us that, even to this day, people denigrate the intrinsic dignity of each human person and go to extreme measures to stamp out civilizations different from their own in the hopeless quest of imposing their religious convictions on the whole of society. Such efforts are doomed to fail, mainly because they are trying to impose values from the outside that most of the people deny and fight against from within. The transformation of society cannot take place from the outside in, but from the inside out. The transformation of society will take place only one heart at a time. Efforts to do otherwise likely end in failure. Such an opinion is simple, common sense. It is not a matter of choosing one side or political party over and against another but of keeping an eye out for the common good.

After 9/11, Americans and the world over mourned the loss of so many innocent people to an act of senseless violence. Just about everyone in the world knows where they were on September 11th of that year. The date has become a marker in the lives of so many people living at that time, and they have passed on the importance of that date to succeeding generations. Just how they have passed that on is another matter. Have we become more open, more understanding, more willing to engage in dialogue with those who have harmed us? Or have we followed their lead and lashed back at them without any effort whatsoever at trying to understand their issues and concerns, their values, and beliefs? Sad to say, the verdict is not yet in. Much remains to be seen.

The mourning that took place on 9/11 was of various kinds. We mourned the loss of those we knew. We grieved over those we did not know yet felt their lives were all too soon unjustly taken from them. We lamented the destruction of the Twin Towers, a symbol of American pride and prosperity. We bowed our heads in horror that human beings could do such a thing to their fellow human beings. And, yes, there was anger. We wanted to lash back. We wanted to bring those responsible for this heinous crime to justice. We wanted a reckoning for the lives taken from us on such short notice and in such a wanton, destructive manner. Words cannot express the feeling of loss and abandonment we felt on that tragic morn.

The first responders were the heroes. They rushed into the burning towers seeking to save others from the pit of destruction. They charged up the stairs in search of life, saved those they could, and lost their own in the process. The mourning on that day had a way of expanding outward to touch even those on the outer perimeters of the crisis. It spread outward in concentric circles from those who died, to their loved ones, to their friends and acquaintances, to those in New York City, Shanksville, Pennsylvania, and Washington, D.C., to the rest of the United States, to its allies in Europe and beyond, and ultimately to the. entire world. Those who rejoiced that such a massive blow could be dealt to their sworn enemies were overshadowed by the outpouring of sentiment that came to America from all corners of the globe.

How will those who mourn the tragedy of 9/11 be comforted? How can the vast emptiness left in the souls who mourn the tragic loss of their loved ones be filled or, at the very least, relieved or in some way alleviated? Little can be said or done in the face of such brutality. Nothing can replace the presence of those whose lives were taken from us all too soon and in such a horrible manner. Their absence in our lives will be with us for the rest of our lives. We will never forget them. We can never forget them. Their deaths are burned in our memories. We carry them with us wherever we go. All we can do is to try to look beneath the pain and ponder what we find there. All we can do is allow our mourning to rise to the surface and lift it up in prayer. Whatever comfort we may experience will come only from above and from those who place their hope in the God who mourns for his children and seeks to comfort them by embracing their death with his very own.

The Cross of Christ

In all the confusion of 9/11, two steel girders in the shape of a cross came into view and gave people hope that God had not abandoned them amid all the chaos.[5] If in the days of ancient Rome, the cross had been a sign of cruelty and death, then Jesus transformed it into one of comfort and

---

[5] Rick Hampson, "Ground Zero Cross, A powerful Symbol for the 9/11 Museum," USA Today, https://www.usatoday.com/story/news/nation/2014/05/13/911-ground-zero-museum-cross-world-trade-center/8907003/.

hope. As Christians, we believe that death, however it comes, be it from cruel, inhuman suffering or in the quiet peace of sleep, does not mark the end of life, but only the beginning. Jesus, we believe, defeated death and did so for our sake. We call ourselves Christians because we have responded to his call to take up our cross and follow him. Just what that cross might be is different for each of us. We bless ourselves and others with the sign of the cross: "In the name of the Father, and of the Son, and of the Holy Spirit." We do so throughout our lives and every time we turn to God in prayer and celebrate the sacraments. This simple prayer reminds us that our mourning, even the horrible grief that befell us on 9/11, will one day end and by transformed by hope into a glorious and resurrected joy. The cross is a sign of comfort to all who believe in Jesus' great love for humanity which led him to stretch out his arms on the cross as his life slowly ebbed from him. The cross, we believe, is the tree of life. It lies at the very center of our faith, rooted in the ground, yet pointed upward, vertically, toward the heavens and stretching horizontally across the sky to embrace the entire human family.

When Jesus hung from the cross, he saw those who reviled him (the Roman soldiers, the priests, the Pharisees) and those who were mourning for him (his mother, Mary Magdalen, Mary, the wife of Clopus, the beloved disciple). Among his last words from the cross, were those directed toward his mother and John, the disciple he loved: "Woman, behold, you son." And then to the beloved disciple: "Here is your mother" (Jn 19:27). These words tell us that, even in his final moment, the midst of his intense suffering, Jesus sought to comfort those who loved and cared for him. "Blessed are those who mourn for they shall be comforted" (Mt 5:4). When Jesus said these words during his Sermon on the Mount, could he have been thinking of his mother as she would mourn him at the foot of the cross and as she watched them lay him in the tomb? Could he have been thinking of his beloved disciple with whom he shared a deep spiritual friendship? Could he have been thinking of all those who suffer the loss of a loved one and have no one to comfort them in their grief and sorrow? Even from the cross, Jesus sought to comfort those who mourn. Those who mourned their loved ones lost on 9/11 can look to the cross and find comfort in the cross of Jesus of Nazareth who gave up his life so that others could have life.

Carrying the Cross

When Jesus says, "Blessed are those who mourn," he is ultimately pointing to the trials of the cross. Most of us have ambivalent feelings about the crosses we are asked to carry in this life. We are told to embrace them yet are also burdened by them. We believe that bearing them is an action that imitates Christ, yet we are fearful that we will fail miserably at doing so. We mourn the loss of life our crosses will ultimately lead us to, and we have hidden doubts about the promise of new life that lies beyond the grave. We mourn our own deaths as we carry our crosses and ultimately hang from them. We also mourn for those who mourn for us and the deep grief and sorrow it causes them.

The only comfort our crosses have to offer is our faith in Christ and his paschal mystery. We carry our crosses not simply because Jesus asks us to but because of our firm conviction that, by embracing his cross wholeheartedly as a manifestation of the Father's love for us, Jesus conquered death and rose from his grave. We follow the way of the cross in the hope that we too may one day look back on our lives and see death not as an end but as a new beginning. The comfort of the cross (its triumph if you will) is the empty tomb. Those who mourn the deaths of their loved ones are comforted by the hope that their tombs will also one day be emptied and that they will be reunited with their loved ones in the afterlife life that is to come.

When seen in this light, Jesus' paschal mystery is a perfect expression on the supernatural level of the twofold anabolic/catabolic movement we find in nature. We may even go so far as to say that what we find in nature is nothing but a vestige or a vague reflection of what exists within God himself. If "God is love," as Scripture tells us (1 Jn 4:8), then the very dynamic of kenotic dying to self and ongoing renewal must somehow exist within the divine nature itself. That is not to say that God experiences decomposition and growth in the same way that we find in nature, but that the underlying downward pattern of selfless love as shown in Jesus' embrace of the cross us is offset by the corresponding upward movement of love of the Father who mourns the death of his Son from above as Mary mourned the death of her Son from below. If Mary is "Our Lady of Sorrows," then the Spirit of the Father, is "The Comforter," who consoles her as she grieves over the loss of her son and us as we suffer the loss of our loved ones.

Conclusion

Jesus knew what it was like to mourn. He was like us in all things but sin and experienced the entire gamut of human emotions, including those of mourning, grief, and sadness. He wept over the fate of Jerusalem (Lk 19:41-44). He wept upon hearing of the death of his friend, Lazarus (Jn 11:35). He sweated drops of blood in the Garden of Gethsemane (Lk 22:44). He cried out from the cross in his hour of desperation (Mt 27:46). He mourns for us whenever we fall under spell of sin and place our souls in deadly danger.

Jesus also knew what it was like to comfort. He consoled the woman caught in adultery (Jn 8:1-11). He encouraged Peter after his shameful denial (Jn 21:15-19). He told his disciples time and again not to be afraid (Mt 28:9-10, Mk 5:36, Mk 6:49-50, Lk 5:10, Jn 6:19-20). He comforted his mother while he was hanging from the cross (Jn 19:26-27). He opens his heart to us whenever we open our own to him in prayer. He accompanies us at the hour of our death and promises to turn our mourning to joy.

The second beatitude reminds us that the sorrows of the present world will one day pass. Our troubles will not simply fade away, however, but will themselves be transformed to something far greater. Those who mourn will be comforted, because the purpose of life is to experience an intimate personal communion with God. To experience God in this way is to live in the Spirit and have the good fortune of experiencing his gifts and fruits. Joy, just one of the many fruits of the

Spirit (Gal 5:22), is the divine remedy for human grief. Jesus promises to comfort those who mourn because he knows that he will send his Spirit to live in and vivify the hearts of those whose hearts are presently filled with sorrow. Just as the Spirit inspired Mary, "Our Lady of Sorrows," to proclaim the greatness of the Lord, so too does he promise to visit us so that our souls also might magnify the Lord and our spirits might rejoice in God our savior (Lk 1:46-47).

The Blessings of the Beatitudes

- Have you ever grieved over the loss of a family member?
- Have you ever mourned over a broken friendship?
- Have you ever comforted someone in such mourning?
- If so, what did it take to do so?
- Has anyone ever comforted you when you were in a state of mourning?
- Will there ever come a time when there will be no need for mourning?

Prayer

Lord, you mourned at the death of Lazarus your friend and comforted Mary and Martha in their grief. Help me to be a comfort to those grieving over the loss of their loved ones. Help me to comfort them and be present to them in such a way that they will know that they must live in the hope of being reunited with those they love. Comfort me in my times of loss and mourning. Help me to live in the hope of the day when all our mourning will come to an end.

Chapter Three

Blessed are the Meek

"Blessed are the meek, for they will inherit the earth" (Mt 5:5). The story is told of how once, many years ago, a bishop, a priest, and a poor peasant were praying in one of Europe's great cathedrals. The bishop approached the altar rail, beat his chest and declared, "I am nothing! I am nothing!" Then the priest approached the altar rail, beat his chest, and declared, "I am nothing! I am nothing!" The humble peasant was deeply moved by these actions, so he approached the altar rail, beat his chest and declared, "I am nothing! I am nothing!" At that, the priest turned in anger and whispered furiously into the bishop's ear, "Who the hell does he think he is?"[1]

It is one thing to speak about humility and quite another to manifest it in one's daily life. Words are one thing: example, quite another. I

---

[1] See, for example, Melinama, Pratie Place Blog, entry posted November 27, 2005, available online at http://pratie.blogspot.com/2005/11/humility.html.

make no claims about my own humility, although I admit that, as a follower of Christ, it is a virtue I wish I had. I should state at the very outset that if you really want to learn something about the subject, you probably would be much better off reading about it in the lives of the saints or praying for it at their tombs than reading to a lengthy tome that can in no way do justice to it.

Via Negativa *and* Via Positiva

Although I cannot say that I know very much about humility from firsthand experience, I do know quite a bit about its contrary vice, that fundamental self-centeredness so deeply ingrained in the human condition that goes by the name of "Pride."

Most of us, I believe, know what humility is by way of negative example, by knowing what it is not. We know what it means to be proud and think of humility as its opposite. St. Bernard of Clairvaux (1090-1153) would very much agree; he wrote an entire treatise on humility by telling us all about pride. He justifies himself in this way: "I can teach only what I have learned….I have nothing to set before you except the order of my descent. But, if you look carefully, you will find there the way up."[2] Even the most egregious of sinners, he seems to be telling us, can teach us something about the way of holiness. Their negative example reveals the signposts of pride which we must carefully avoid and gives us an indication of what it would be like to walk the way of humility. If pride is the "mother of all vice," as Bernard is telling us, then humility must be closely linked to charity, which Thomas Aquinas identifies as the "mother of all virtue."[3]

Thank God, however, that we need not rely solely on the *via negativa* to learn about humility. Throughout history he has raised up holy men and women of whose lives of dedicated love and service have given us concrete indications of what

---

[2] Bernard of Clairvaux, *On the Steps of Humility and Pride*, XXII.57 in *Bernard of Clairvaux: Selected Works*, trans. G. R. Evans, The Classics of Western Spirituality (New York/Mahwah, NJ: Paulist Press, 1987), 142.

[3] See Thomas Aquinas, *Summa theologiae* (Sth), II-II, q. 23, a. 8, ad 3m.

it means to walk the way of humility: St. Benedict of Nursia (480-547), St. Francis of Assisi (1181/82-1226), St. Teresa of Avila (1515-1582), St. Philip Neri (1515-1595), St. Thérèse of Lisieux (1873-1897), Blessed Charles de Foucauld (1858-1916), Blessed Teresa of Calcutta (1910-1997)—to name but a few. Our Blessed Mother, no doubt, offers us the clearest example. In *The Glories of Mary*, St. Alphonsus Liguori (1696-1787) tells us that "Since [she] was the first and most perfect disciple of Jesus in the practice of the virtues, she naturally excelled in the practice of humility."[4] Her humble *fiat* to the Lord reveals the depths of her love for God and her desire to do his will no matter what the cost. *The Magnificat,* her great hymn of praise which has become so important to the Church's daily prayer, speaks of how God has "looked with favor upon his servant in her lowliness" and "confused the proud in their inmost thoughts" (Lk 1:48, 51). Mary's humility permeates her entire life and should be reflected in simi-

---

[4] Alphonsus de Liguori, *The Glories of Mary* (Liguori, MO: Liguori Publications, 1963; 2000 revised ed.), 329.

lar ways also in ours. Unless we are humble, we can never be considered true children of Mary.

Christ's Downward Pull

Even Mary's humility, however, pales in comparison with the fruit of her womb. Her holiness is purely derivative, in much the same way that the moon gives off light that it receives from the sun. If we wish to go to the source of humility, we need to look to the example of her Son, who from all eternity empties himself in obedience to the will of the Father. The Apostle Paul describes this process of kenotic self-emptying in the famous Christological hymn that is preserved in his letter to the Philippians 2:6-11, which reads as follows:

> Though he was in the form of God,
> he did not deem equality with God
> something to be grasped at.
> Rather, he emptied himself
> and took the form of a slave,
> being born in the likeness of men.
> He was known to be of human estate,

and it was thus that he humbled himself,
obediently accepting even death,
death on a cross!
Because of this,
God highly exalted him
and bestowed on him the name
above every other name,
So that at Jesus' name
every knee must bend
in the heavens, on the earth,
and under the earth,
and every tongue proclaim
to the glory of God the Father:
JESUS CHRIST IS LORD!

As this ancient Christian hymn indicates, Christ's humility is intimately tied to his obedience to the Father. Equality with God is not something to cling to and be exploited for personal ends, but to be used in loving service for the good and well-being of others. In a collaborative work on the nature of compassion, the late Henri J. M. Nouwen (1932-1996) refers to this as the great "downward pull" of Christ's salvific mission, one that encompasses the great mysteries of his life, death, and resurrection.[5] Rather than striving to put himself first, he sought to serve others and did so by placing himself last. He emptied his soul of all concern for self and filled it instead with a deep concern for others. This orientation towards others lies at the very heart of Jesus' life and mission.

This downward Christological pull, as we have seen, has been described as a fourfold process of self-emptying: (1) The Word of God entered our world, (2) gave of himself completely, (3) became our nourishment, and (4) the source of our hope. Taken as a whole, this process represents a single event of both historical and transcendent significance that occurs both in and out of time, in one age, and in every age, from now unto eternity. Taken individually, these various stages or steps correspond to different aspects of the one mystery of Christ: the first, to his incarnation; the second, to his earthly life and death; the third, to his insti-

---

[5] Donald P. McNeill, Douglas A. Morrison, and Henri J. M. Nouwen, *Compassion: A Reflection on the Christian Life* (Garden City, NY: Doubleday, 1982), 27-28.

tution of the Eucharist; the fourth, to his resurrection. A more precise description of the process would thus read: *Christ came to us in his incarnation, gave of himself completely in both his living and his dying, gave us in the Eucharist the nourishment of his own body and blood, and promised us in his resurrection the life of a transformed humanity.*[6] God loved us so much that he poured himself into our humanity, into the warp and woof of our daily lives, into the very food we eat, so that we might one day become like him. "God became human," as we have seen, "so that humanity might become divine."

When seen in this light, humility lies at the very heart of Jesus' self-understanding. He defines himself in terms of his selfless obedience to the will of the Father. He who is "meek and humble of heart" makes the Father's will his own and seeks to carry it out with all his heart and soul. Humility, for Jesus, is more than merely placing the concerns of the Father before his own as if there were a difference between the two. Jesus does not merely conform his will to that of his Father, but com-

---

[6] See Billy, *Evangelical Kernels*, 17-31.

pletely identifies with it. The two are so close that their wills are virtually are one and the same. "The Father and I are one," he tells us (Jn 10:30). For the Son, this absolute union with the Father's will exists from all eternity and lies at the heart of the "downward pull" that typifies Jesus' redemptive mission.

Blessings of the Kingdom

Some of you may be wondering how this "downward pull" specifically manifested itself in Jesus' mind and heart and in those of his followers—and with good reason. It is one thing to speak in general terms of loving others and placing their needs before our own, and quite another to talk about the concrete qualities present within us that make such actions possible. As Christians, we are fortunate in having the words of the Beatitudes, a series of eight words or phrases that represents Jesus' attempt to convey to his followers the values of the kingdom he has come to proclaim. Theologians such as Augustine of Hippo (354-430) and Thomas Aquinas (1224/25-1274) see the Beatitudes as Jesus' understanding of what it means to be "happy" or "blessed" and, for this reason, place them at the very heart of Christian ethics. It is also worth noting that both Augustine and Aquinas draw a close connection between the Beatitudes and the Gifts of the Holy Spirit. In doing so, they emphasize that humility and its associated virtues are not something that we do through our own efforts, but that God accomplishes in us through the work of his Spirit.[7]

The problem with the Beatitudes, however, is that they have become so familiar to us over the years that we can easily overlook the powerful message they seek to convey. Over forty years ago, J. B. Phillips (1906-1982), an Anglican minister probably best known as the translator of *The New Testament in Modern English*, sought to rectify this situation by contrasting the different mindsets of those who dwell in Christ's heart and those who do not. His version of these opposing world

---

[7] For a treatment of Augustine's and Aquinas's teaching on the Beatitudes and the Gifts, see Pinckaers, *The Sources of Christian Ethics*, 151-58.

views—of the Beatitudes and the Woes—goes like this:

Most people think:

Happy are the pushers, for they get on in the world.

Happy are the hard-boiled, for they never let life hurt them.

Happy are they who complain, for they get their own way in the end.

Happy are the blasé, for they never worry over their sins.

Happy are the slave-drivers, for they get results.

Happy are the knowledgeable men of the world, for they know their way around.

Happy are the trouble-makers, for people have to take notice of them.

Jesus Christ said:

Happy are those who realize their spiritual poverty; they have already entered the kingdom of Reality.

Happy are they who bear their share of the world's pain; in the long run they will know more happiness than those who avoid it.

Happy are those who accept life and their own limitations; they will find more in life than anybody.

Happy are those who long to be truly "good;" they will fully realize their ambition.

Happy are those who are ready to make allowances and to forgive; they will know the love of God.

Happy are those who are real in their thoughts and feelings; in the end they will see the ultimate Reality, God.

Happy are those who help others to live together; they will be known to be doing God's work.[8]

Phillips maintains that the poetic form and outdated language of the Beatitudes prevents us

---

[8] J. B. Phillips, *Your God Is Too Small* (New York: Macmillan, 1967), 92-93.

from seeing their true revolutionary character. Jesus came into this world to revolutionize the hearts of his followers. We find happiness (beatitude, heaven) by dwelling in his heart and by allowing his Spirit to dwell in ours. We do this not through our own efforts, but by humbly coming to the Lord and inviting him into our hearts.

The document of the Pontifical Biblical Commission, *The Bible and Morality: Biblical Roots and Christian Conduct*, emphasizes this radical nature of the beatitudes:

> From the very beginning the beatitudes place morality in a radical context. They affirm paradoxically the fundamental dignity of the human being in the person of the most disadvantaged, whom God defends in a preferential manner: the poor, the afflicted, the meek, the hungry, the persecuted. They are 'sons of God (v. 9), heirs of the kingdom of God (vv. 3, 10). Jesus himself typifies, in a most radical way, the 'poor' (Mt 8:19; cf. 2 Cor 8:9; Phil 2:6-8), the 'meek and humble' (Mt 11:29) and 'perse-

cuted for righteousness' sake.'[9]

These sayings, the Commission maintains, are meant for everyone, not a select few. They "are not to be seen as inaccessible ideals," but "reflect the characteristics of the sons and daughters of God in the fullness of the kingdom." "They provide a basic outlook to lead the disciple to seek and find similar ways of regulating actions and values towards the final vision of the gospel, to lead a better life in the world, in anticipation of the coming of the kingdom."[10]

The Practice of Humility

By now it should be manifestly clear that being humble does not simply happen. It involves a long, arduous process that can take an entire lifetime to bear results. At the outset, we must fight

---

[9] Pontifical Biblical Commission, *The Bible and Morality: Biblical Roots of Christian Conduct*, no. 101 (Vatican City: Libreria Editrice Vaticana, 2008), 138.

[10] Ibid., 142. For the spectrum of interpretation given to the Beatitudes, see Pinckaers, *The Sources of Christian Ethics*, 134-39.

against the sin of pride, that tendency toward self-centeredness within of each of us that exaggerates our sense of importance and self-worth. This tendency must be constantly kept in check, for it is a deep spiritual wound that never fully goes away during our earthly sojourn.

The main character of C. S. Lewis's (1898-1963) *The Screwtape Letters*, a master devil named Screwtape, who writes a series of letters to his inexperienced nephew, Wormwood, on how to lead a human being successfully down the road to perdition, reveals the kind of circular mind traps that can all too easily turn humility back into pride.

I see only one thing to do at the moment. Your patient has become humble; have you drawn his attention to the fact? All virtues are less formidable to us once the man is aware that he has them, but this is specially true of humility. Catch him at the moment when he is really poor in spirit and smuggle into his mind the gratifying reflection, "By jove! I'm being humble," and almost immediately pride—pride at his own humility—will appear. If he awakes to the danger and tries to smother this new form of pride, make him proud of his attempt—and so on, through as many stages as you please. But don't try this too long, for fear you awake his sense of humour and proportion, in which case he will merely laugh at you and go to bed.[11]

Screwtape is a master of human psychology and knows how to trick someone into doing his bidding without even realizing it. He knows when to speak and when to remain silent, when to push and when to pull. In the end, he counsels Wormwood to defeat humility with falsehood:

> The great thing is to make him value an opinion for some quality other than truth, thus introducing an element of dishonesty and make-believe into the heart of what otherwise threatens to become a virtue. By this method thousands of humans have been brought to think that humility means pretty women try-

---

[11] C. S. Lewis, *The Screwtape Letters* (New York: Macmillan, 1961; revised paperback ed., 1982), 62-63.

ing to believe they are ugly and clever men trying to believe they are fools. And since what
they are trying to believe may, in some cases,
be manifest nonsense, they cannot succeed in
believing it, and we have the chance of keeping
their minds endlessly revolving on themselves
in an effort to achieve the impossible.[12]

You may have heard of the distinction commonly made in books of Christian spirituality between True Self and False Self.[13] The first rests on
a true evaluation of the self; the second, on illu-
sion and self-deceit. The True Self reveals a person's true identity; the False Self, nothing but a
smokescreen of lies and falsehoods. In a similar
way, there is true humility and false humility: the
first rejoices in one's gifts and talents; the second,
belittles or demeans them. According to Thomas
Merton: "There is a false humility which thinks it
is pride to desire the highest greatness—the perfection of contemplation, the summit of mystical

---

[12] Ibid., 64

[13] See, for example, Thomas Merton, *No Man Is an
Island* (Garden City, NY: Image Books,1967), 155.

union with God. This is one of the biggest illusions in the spiritual life because it is only in this
greatness, only in this exalted union, that we can
achieve perfect humility."[14] Whenever he can,
Screwtape tries to turn true humility into false.
God— "the Enemy," as Screwtape calls him—has
an entirely different goal.

> The Enemy [says Screwtape] wants to bring
> the man to a state of mind in which he could
> design the best cathedral in the world, and
> know it to be the best, and rejoice in the fact,
> without being any more (or less) or otherwise
> glad at having done it than he would be if it
> had been done by another. The Enemy wants
> him, in the end, to be so free from any bias in
> his own favor that he can rejoice in his own
> talents as frankly and gratefully as in his
> neighbor's talents—or in a sunrise, an ele-
> phant, or a waterfall. He wants each man, in
> the long run, to be able to recognize all crea-
> tures (even himself) as glorious and excellent

---

[14] Thomas Merton, *Seeds of Contemplation* (London: The Catholic Book Club, 1950), 109-10.

things. He wants to kill their animal self-love as soon as possible; but it is His long-term policy, I fear, to restore to them a new kind of self-love—a charity and gratitude for all selves, including their own; when they have really learned to love their neighbors as themselves, they will be allowed to love themselves as their neighbors. For we must never forget what is the most repellent and inexplicable trait in our Enemy; He *really* loves the hairless bipeds He has created, and always gives back to them with His right hand what He has taken away with His left.[15]

As we mature in spiritual life, we gradually become more and more "other-centered." One important help in this transition from pride to humility is meditating on the example given us to by the Lord himself in his incarnation, hidden life, public ministry, passion and death, and Eucharistic life. The words of Mr. Blue, the twentieth-century poverello from the novel by Myles Connolly (1897-1964) by the same name, come to

---

[15] Lewis, *The Screwtape Letters,* 64-65.

mind as he stares out on the immensity of space
on a cold, dark night:

I think…my heart would break with all this
immensity if I did not know that God Himself
once stood beneath it, a young man, as small
as I….Did it ever occur to you that it was
Christ Who humanized infinitude, so to
speak? When God became man, He made you
and me and the rest of us pretty important
people. He not only redeemed us. He saved us
from the terrible burden of infinity….My
hands, my feet, my poor little brain, my eyes,
my ears, all matter more than the whole sweep
of these constellations!…God Himself, the God
to Whom this whole universe-specked display
is as nothing, God Himself had hands like
mine and feet like mine, and eyes, and brain,
and ears!….Without Christ we would be little
more than bacteria breeding on a pebble in
space, or glints of ideas in a whirling void of
abstractions. Because of Him, I can stand here
out under this cold immensity and know that
my infinitesimal pulse-beats and acts and

thoughts are of more importance than this whole show of a universe. Only for Him, I would be crushed beneath the weight of all these worlds. Only for Him, I would tumble dazed into the gaping chasms of space and time. Only for Him, I would be confounded before the awful fertility and intricacy of all life. Only for Him, I would be the merest of animalcules crawling on the merest of motes in a frigid Infinity….But behold…behold! God wept and laughed and dined and wined and suffered and died even as you and I. Blah!—for the immensity of space! Blah! —for those who would have me a microcosm in the meaningless tangle of an endless evolution! I am no microcosm. I, too, am a Son of God.[16]

"Humility is truth," we are often told. Mr. Blue invites us to take this humble truth to heart by taking a good hard look at Jesus and what his existence means for us. He asks us to reflect on how God's Son emptied himself into the womb of a

---

[16] Myles Connolly, *Mr. Blue* (Garden City, NY: Image Books, 1954), 39-41.

woman to become one of us. He invites us to
ponder the impoverished circumstances sur-
rounding Jesus' birth and to the many years he
spent growing up in a small backwater village in
Galilee. He bids us to think of how he placed others before himself in his ministry of teaching and
healing and as he preached the coming of the
kingdom. He asks us to consider his silent sub-
mission as he was delivered into the hands of his
enemies, suffered cruel and inhuman torture, and
death by crucifixion. We also look to how he
pours himself into the elements of bread and wine
and remains hidden there in all the tabernacles of
the world to comfort us, strengthen us, and inspire us.

Conclusion

Walking humbly in an unbelieving world has
to do with trying to become ourselves in our faith.
It means wanting to become what we are in God's
eyes and nothing more. This journey is essentially
an interior one that involves stripping ourselves of
the values of the world and adhering more and

more closely to those of the kingdom. It is a journey of faith that unfolds in the present yet is firmly oriented toward the future. Since Jesus himself told us that his kingdom was not of this world, it follows that the very values upon which that kingdom is built must possess a transcendent, otherworldly character and should be clearly manifest in the lives of his followers.

Jesus' life and actions inspire us to embrace those values. The emptying of self that defined his life must, in some way, also be reflected in our own. We do so in a variety of ways and in several different directions. For example, we practice humility toward God by honoring him as the source of all goodness, thanking him for all the gifts he has given us, and fostering a sense of dependence on him in all things. We practice humility toward our neighbors by seeing all the good in them as coming from God, rejoicing in their virtues and accomplishments, and praying for their conversion when they display their faults and weaknesses. We practice humility toward ourselves by thanking God for all the good in us, not drawing attention to ourselves, and opening our hearts in service to others.

What does it mean to walk humbly in an un-believing world? It means that, like Jesus, we are called to enter the world of those around us, give ourselves to them completely, to the point of be-coming nourishment for them, and a source of hope. It means participating in the downward pull that characterized his life and which must eventu-ally be embraced as the defining principle of our own. It means taking Jesus' words to his Father in heaven to heart, "your kingdom come, your will be done one earth as it is in heaven" (Mt 6:10). It means following Christ with the hope of one day becoming our truest, deepest selves. It means em-bracing and rejoicing in our various gifts and tal-ents, while, at the same time, walking the way of becoming a selfless self, someone entirely centered on God, who lives for others, and who does not give oneself a second thought.

The Blessings of the Beatitudes

- Why is it so difficult to be humble?
- What is it within us that makes it so hard to be so?
- In what ways was Jesus meek and humble of heart?
- Do you want to be like Jesus?
- Do you want to be meek and humble of heart?
- Why will the meek inherit the earth?

Prayer

Lord, you are "the way, he truth, and the life" (Jn 14:16). Humility is truth. Help me to live in the truth. Help me to life out of my true self rather than my false self. Help me to overcome my illusions of grandeur and greatness. Help to see myself for who and what I truly am, a sinner in constant need of repentance, someone who must always rely on you. You humbled yourself by emptying your divinity into our humanity. Help me to follow you along the way of humility.

Chapter Four

Blessed are those who Hunger and Thirst after Righteousness

"Blessed are those who hunger and thirst for righteousness, for they will be filled" (Mt 5:6). In the fourth beatitude, Jesus speaks about an attitude of heart that longs for righteousness. A righteous person is just. Yearning for justice—the deeply rooted concern that everyone receives what is due to him or her (be it oneself, one's neighbor, or God) is a true mark of the just person. Those who hunger and thirst for righteousness seek what is due them on every level of their human makeup: the physical, psychological (and intellectual), spiritual, and social. Such a yearning involves a person's interior life (on all its various levels), his or her relationships with others, and ultimately his or her relationship with God. When Jesus says that those who hunger and thirst for righteousness will be satisfied, he is saying that they will ultimately see the realization of the kingdom of God in their midst. He promises them that their yearning for righteousness will one day be quenched. He tells them that what *they* seek Jesus, our Lord, *also* seeks, because he is the Word of God, and he and the Father are one. Where can we find such individuals, those who seek to relate to others in a way that recognizes their unique character and way of being in the world and, at the same time, yearn for giving everyone one his or her due? The Gospels give us a perfect example of such a person in the figure of St. Joseph, the foster father of Jesus, or, to use a more recent distinction, the natural (as opposed to biological) father of Jesus.[1]

Joseph, the Just Man

Justice is a virtue, one of the four cardinal virtues. It is a disposition of the soul, in this case the power of the will to give everyone what is due them. Justice can be natural or infused. When it is

---

[1] For the distinction between the biological and natural father, see Carter Griffin, *Why Celibacy? Reclaiming the Fatherhood of the Priest* (Steubenville, OH: Emmaus Road, 2019), 15-21.

natural, it gives all things—creation, our family, and friends, ourselves— what is due to them on a natural level. When it is infused, that is, when it is informed by grace, it is oriented toward the supernatural in such a way that everything in one's life is oriented toward God. In other words, when justice is infused, we give God, creation, our family, friends, ourselves, and even God what is due to them because we recognize that we all have the same end: the *visio Dei*, that is, the vision of God. St. Joseph, the natural husband of Mary and the foster father of Jesus is the example par excellence of the "Just Man." He is someone who has exhibited deep within his soul all the qualities of the virtue of justice, that disposition of the soul that strives to give everyone his or her due.

Matthew's Gospel describes Joseph as "a righteous man" (Mt 1:19). He did not wish to shame Mary by breaking off their betrothal once he discovered that she was with child outside of wedlock and that the child was not his own. His own intention was reaffirmed when an angel of the Lord appeared to him in a dream, telling him not to be afraid to take Mary as his wife, since she had con-

ceived by the power of the Holy Spirit and the
child, who was to be named Jesus, would save the
people from their sins (Mt 1:20-22). All this was
done to fulfill the prophecy in Isaiah that a virgin
would conceive and bear a child who was to be
called Emmanuel, which means, "God is with us"
(Mt 1:24).

Joseph, in other words, was a man who listened to his own heart, as well as to the promptings of the Spirit speaking to him in his dreams.
He discounted neither, took them seriously, and
acted on them, taking Mary as his wife, protecting
her and the child she bore, and treating Jesus as
his own son. Joseph was a righteous man, a just
man, a quiet man. The Gospels do not record a
single word ever uttered from his lips. As head of
his household, he provided for, protected, and
guided his wife and child, giving them a loving
environment in which they could grow and prosper. He worked by the sweat of his brow and gave
the savior of the world a home where he could
grow and prosper. If Mary is the "Ark of the Cov-
enant," Joseph provided the tent that housed it,
first in Bethlehem, then in Egypt when the holy

family fled from Herod's henchmen, and finally in Nazareth. "Can anything good come from Nazareth?" (Jn 1:46). These words spoken by Nathanael in the Gospel of John remind us that Nazareth was a backwater town of Galilee that had little (if any) prominence in Jewish history. That God chose to enter our world through the womb of Mary and under the protection of Joseph, reminds us of his predilection for the poor and marginalized. Joseph's righteousness, in other words, reflects the justice and mercy of God. His hunger and thirst for righteousness was satisfied in the love he bore for his family and the way he gave himself to them throughout his life until the day he died.

Yearning for Justice

To hunger and thirst for justice means more than stiving to uproot the many injustices that plague human society. A disordered society stems from disorder in the human soul. Disarray in the without, as the Cardinal Ratzinger points out, reflects the disarray within the human heart: "[T]he pollution of the outward environment that we are witnessing is only the mirror and the consequence of the pollution of the inward environment, to which we pay too little heed."[2] The evils and injustices in the outer world stem from the evils and injustices of the human soul. Its transformation will ultimately come about by changing people's hearts and minds, not merely by enacting legislation that keeps order in society. Laws are only as good as their makers. There will continue to be injustices in society if human beings allow the darkness of evil to influence their attitudes, words, laws, and actions. The macrocosm of human society, in other words, reflects the microcosm of the human soul.

Justice is first and foremost a virtue. On the natural level, it is an acquired disposition of the will (i.e., the soul's intellectual appetite) that seeks to give others their due. When it is infused by grace it focuses entirely on God and seeks to give

---

[2] Joseph Cardinal Ratzinger, *Salt oof the Earth: The Church at the End of the Millennium, an Interview with Peter Seewald* (San Francisco: Ignatius Press, 1997), 230-31.

him and, because of him, others what rightfully belongs to them. For God, this means following his commandment of love and rendering him glory and honor and praise in divine worship. For others, it means treating them with respect and recognizing their inherent dignity and rights by virtue of their being created in God's image and likeness. The Holy Spirit then perfects this infused disposition of the will by enabling a person to respond spontaneously to his just and pious promptings. The truly just and pious person is someone who sees everything in the light of God's creative, redemptive, and sanctifying action in the world. Such a person sees that, when all is said and done, it is God alone who brings justice to the world, and he chooses to do so by living in people's hearts and transforming society one heart at a time.

Social justice is intimately related to interior righteousness. If everyone's souls were properly ordered, society itself would follow suit. The challenge is to concentrate all our efforts on transforming the human heart. Joseph, the husband of Mary, the foster (or what today we would say is the "natural" as opposed to the "biological" father of Jesus) was a righteous man, a just man, someone who gave everyone their due and who was open and free enough to listen to the promptings of the Spirit in his life. It was this inner disposition of righteousness and justice that led him to lead his family out of the treacherous hands of Herod's henchmen and take his family out of danger and int Egypt. This natural (adoptive) father of Jesus took the savior of the world from the very clutches of a civilization that had oppressed his countrymen so many years before. The narrative of the Gospel tells us that Joseph, in listening to the Holy Spirit in his dreams, recognized what was being said, understood what was being asked of him, and acted upon it. He is the exemplar par excellence of the just man, of someone whose virtuous life eventually led to the transformation of society.

Becoming Just, Becoming Holy.

The virtues all coinhere. Being just also entails being prudent, courageous, temperate faithful, hopeful, and loving. When they are infused by

God's grace, these virtues orient us toward God, who causes our existence, sustains us in being, and calls us to himself as our final end. The just person is ultimately called to live a life of holiness, so that he or she might one day see God face-to-face in the beatific vision. When Jesus says, "Blessed are they who hunger and thirst for right-eousness, for they will be satisfied," he is remind-ing his hearers that the satisfaction of such long-ing does not come about by human effort alone, but only with God's help. "They shall be satisfied," implies that what they yearn for will be given to them by the loving assistance of God's grace. Their yearning for justice is itself a gift from God, a holy longing, the ultimate fulfillment of which is a work of divine providence in which humans merely participate.

The just person hungers and thirsts for the justice of God, which culminates in Jesus' paschal mystery. His passion and death, resurrection, and ascension are all an expression of the Divine Mer-cy. As Anselm of Canterbury reminds us in his *Cur Deus homo*, in Christ's death on the cross,

God's justice is satisfied by God's mercy.[3] Adam's sin was of an infinite magnitude and could only by forgiven by a sacrificial death of like proportions. Jesus, the Word of God and Son of the Father, became man and suffered death to satisfy God's justice. The mercy of the Father, in turn, raised him up and elevated humanity to an even higher level of existence. When seen in this light, Jesus is the just man par excellence, someone who reflects the merciful face of the Father and who extends the invitation to his followers to share in the intimate relationship he has with him.

Jesus said to his disciples, "If any wish to become my followers, let them deny themselves and take up their cross and follow me" (Mt 16:24). Following Jesus means embracing the sufferings we encounter in our journey through life and embracing them in the same selfless, self-emptying way that Jesus did. It means viewing them as a sharing in Christ's own redemptive suffering through which God's mercy overcame the ravages of sin and death to enable us to share in the inti-

---

[3] Anselm of Canterbury, *Why God Became Man*, 2.20.

mate life of God himself. Like Jesus, we too are called to enter the world of those around us, give ourselves completely to them through a life of selfless service, and, at times, even to the point of death, become nourishment for them, and a source of hope. Like him, we are called to reflect the merciful face of the Father to men and women everywhere. We will not be shown mercy if we are not merciful to others. We will not share in the divine life, if we fail to follow the way of the Lord Jesus, the way of compassion and forgiveness, the way of a self-emptying giving of self: "For those who wish to save their life will lose it, and those who lose their life for my sake will find it but for my sake whoever loses his life for my sake will find it" (Mt 16:25). Justice and holiness go hand in hand.

A Just Mercy and a Merciful Justice

To hunger and thirst for righteousness is a prerequisite for membership in God's kingdom. What follows are some further remarks about the meaning of the beatitude and its relationship to

Christ, the Church, and the societal well-being of the human family.

To begin with, those who hunger and thirst for righteousness seek the kingdom of God which, at one and the same time, is both within them and in their midst. When Jesus talked to his disciples in this way (Lk 17:21), he was referring to himself. Although he stood in their midst, he also dwelled within their hearts in a deep bond of friendship. These two ways of being present to them reveal a great deal about what yearning for justice is all about. Although the two are intimately related and mutually inform one another, a priority must go to the need for inner conversion and the transformation of the human heart. A truly just society will never come about if there are divided and vicious hearts with which to contend. All human cultures are a product of flawed human minds and hearts. Even the Church, the mystical body of Christ, is both human and divine. It has flaws and weaknesses that will not be completely uprooted until the Lord brings history to a close and heralds the coming of a new heaven and a new earth at the time of his Second Coming.

There are different levels of righteousness. As mentioned above, Jesus is the just man par excellence. He is the New Adam, the Alpha and Omega, the First and Last, the Beginning and the End. He is justice incarnate and it is through him that all other human beings are justified in and through his bleed. Mary, his mother, is the New Eve, the woman who gave birth to her Son by responding with her humble fiat to the angel's message that she would conceive by the Holy Spirit. Conceived free of the stain of original sin by the power of Christ's redemptive action acting retroactively through history, she was completely justified from the first moment of her existence. Joseph, her husband, represents the kind of righteousness available to the rest of humanity. Although conceived in sin and a sinner like the rest of us, he cooperated with the grace of the Holy Spirit, listened to his promptings in his dreams as well as when awake, and served as the protector, guide, and provider of the Holy Family all during Jesus' childhood and formative years. If John the Baptist, represents the thirst of Israel for the coming of the Messiah, then Joseph, Jesus' foster father, represents the welcome given the Messiah when he entered our world as "Emmanuel, which means, 'God is with us'" (Mt 1:23).

Those who yearn for justice and righteousness do so because they sense the lack of it in their present circumstances. The powerful sway of evil in our lives causes us to perpetuate the hold of sin over the world. Even though Jesus conquered death on Easter morning, the struggle between spirit and flesh continues in our lives to this very day. This battle can be won only through faith in Christ, the power of prayer, and living in communion with the Spirit of Christ and the Church that he lives in and vivifies. Each of us is in a different place in our spiritual journey. For some, the hold of sin predominates; for others it has loosened its grasp; for still others its tinder (*fomes peccatis*) is nearly exhausted and perhaps even extinguished. We can conquer the presence of evil in our lives and in society only by picking up our crosses and following Jesus in his journey of selfless service and kenotic self-emptying. That journey follows the ways of purgation, illumination, and union. The first involves keeping God's commandments; the second, the life of virtue; and the third, living life in the Spirit and his manifold gifts. Those who are not on the journey will continue to perpetuate evil in their own lives and in those around them. Those who are on the journey will experience the yearning for righteousness until evil is completely rooted from their lives and they have reached their journey's end.

To hunger and thirst for righteousness's sake involves an implicit understanding that such yearnings will not be satisfied until history draws to a close and the kingdom of God is fully established with Christ's second coming. The yearning for justice points to a final judgment, a separation of the sheep from the goats, the weeds from the wheat, the good from the bad, the saved from the damned. During our present earthly sojourn, the weeds that have been sown by the enemy, are allowed to grow up together with the wheat. Only at harvest time will everything be gathered up, separated, and dealt with accordingly. The satisfaction of one's yearning for justice and righteousness (in this world and the next) comes about not through human effort alone but by the action of God himself acting through them. As history unfolds, the followers of Christ, those who form a part of his mystical body, are granted the honor and privilege of sharing in his paschal mystery and, in doing so, participating in his redemptive suffering, death, and resurrection. Through them, Christ continues to suffer and die for the sins of the world. Through them, he carries on the salvific mission that he began when he entered our world from the womb of the Virgin Mary. Although it was not necessary for God to do this, he did so out of his deep love for humanity and because he truly treats them as his adopted sons and daughters.

Finally, justice reaches its fulfillment in mercy, both of which complement each other and are expressions of an authentic, selfless love. A just person seeks to give everyone their due in order reestablish order first in human society and then in the human heart. The merciful person, by way of contrast, forgives first in the hope of reestablishing order within the evildoer's soul which, in turn, will have an impact on society. A justice that merely seeks to express one's wrath and extract vengeance, is not justice at all but a poor (one might say, "counterfeit") imitation of it. A forgiveness that focuses solely on outward signs but does not penetrate the heart to effect genuine reconciliation is a shallow (even false) expression. If justice is the bare minimum requirement of love, mercy is its fullest expression. For us, justice and mercy exist in tension with one another. For this reason, justice often needs to be tempered by mercy, and mercy, in turn, must seek out the basic requirements of justice. Only in God do the two live and work together in perfect harmony. Those who follow the way of the Lord, Jesus, understand that, by reason of his incarnation and paschal mystery, God's justice was satisfied by God's mercy—and vice versa. When seen in this light, to hunger and thirst for righteousness means that, when living in Christ and with Christ living in us, justice combines with mercy in such a way that both the human heart and human society are properly ordered under the gentle rule of reason's reign. The kingdom of God, in other words, requires both a just mercy and merciful justice. The two go hand in hand.

Conclusion

To hunger and thirst for righteousness is to yearn for the coming of God's kingdom. Those who do so will be satisfied not through their own efforts but because they have opened themselves up to the movement of God's grace in their lives. Such openness brings order to the soul that enlightens the mind, strengthens the will, captures the imagination, and heals the memory. It also tames the passions and brings them under the gentle rule of reason's reign.

The just soul is a virtuous soul, someone who, like St. Joseph, listens to the Spirit's promptings in his life and strives to do what is right for no other reason than that it is simply the right thing to do. It is through men and women such as these that a truly just and virtuous society is conceived, takes root, and flourishes. The kingdom comes through the grace-filled efforts of those who hunger and thirst for righteousness. Through such yearning the kingdom breaks into our world, inhabits it, and transforms it from the inside out.

The fourth beatitude is a reminder to all of us that justice has implications for both the microcosm and the macrocosm, the inner world and the outer world, the life of virtue and that of a just society. In the end, it is only God himself who can bring order to our disordered souls and chaotic world in which we live. It is only by recognizing our dire need for him, opening our hearts to his grace, and responding freely to the gently promptings of his Spirit that our hunger and thirst for righteousness will ultimately be satisfied. It is Jesus, the Lord of history and the Prince of Peace, who will bring peace, the tranquility of order (*tranquillitas ordinis*) to our hearts and to the world in which we live. Those who hunger and thirst for righteousness yearn for the coming of the kingdom of Christ who has come, is come, and is still to come in his glorious fullness at the end of time.

The Blessings of the Beatitudes

- What is righteousness?
- Is it something internal or external?

- Do you yearn for justice?
- Do you hunger and thirst for righteousness?
- Will you ever find either one in this life?
- Do you hope to find them in the life to come?

Prayer

Lord, you are the source of all justice and righteousness. Help me to be a just man, someone who gives everyone their due, someone like Joseph, your foster father, who protected you, provided for you, and guided you in your early years of life. Help me to be shaped in the same way you were shaped in your early years, and as your parents watched you grow in wisdom and knowledge. Help me, Lord. Help me to hunger and thirst for righteousness.

Chapter Five

Blessed are the Merciful

"Blessed are the merciful, for they will receive mercy" (Mt 5:7). When I hear the word, "compassion," I often think of another unfortunate traveler in dire need of roadside assistance, the man who fell prey to robbers in Jesus' parable of the Good Samaritan (Lk 10:25-37). We all know the story and it hardly bears repeating. A man was making his way from Jerusalem to Jericho and is ambushed, stripped, beaten, robbed, and left on the side of the road to die. Two of his own Jewish countrymen see him yet pass him by without lifting a finger to help. It is only a stranger, a lowly Samaritan, who takes pity on him and comes to his aid.

What strikes me most about the parable is that Jesus identifies a priest and a Levite, two members of the priestly tribe of Levi, as those lacking compassion. It may well be that these men thought they were serving God by avoiding the man out of fear of becoming unclean and hence unfit to perform their ritual temple duties in Jerusalem. Such a reason, however, does not excuse them and makes the lesson of Jesus' parable even more powerful. Compassion, he is telling us, is a fundamental quality of Christian discipleship. In his kingdom, everyone is our neighbor. In his kingdom, compassion is the law of the land. The citizens of his kingdom must be men and women of compassion, men and women of forgiveness. If they are not, then they simply are not following the way of the Lord Jesus.

Simply put: Today's disciples are called to think, speak, and act in conformity with the example of Jesus.[1] If they do not, then there is a gap between who they are and who Jesus is calling them to become. The question before us is whether the gap is getting larger or smaller. Most of us would admit that, to some extent, such a gap *does* exist in our lives and would explain it in terms of personal weakness and our own human sinful-

---

[1] Acting in conformity with the example of Jesus is one of the fundamental Biblical criteria for moral reflection. See Pontifical Biblical Commission, *The Bible and Morality*, 137-41.

ness. Most of us would also admit that we sincerely desire to bring the compassionate love of Christ to those we serve.

Christ's Compassion, Christ's Passion

In Christian spirituality, the word "compassion" has many nuances and is difficult to pin down. Although it is often identified with such terms as "mercy," "pity," and "tenderness," its distinct meaning is to express "the empathetic attachment of one being to another."[2] It has been described as "the capacity to be attracted and moved by the fragility, weakness, and suffering of another."[3] Compassion, which comes from the Latin *compassio*, meaning "to suffer with," is "the ability to be vulnerable enough to undergo risk and loss for the good of the other."[4] It is not merely helping another person or group of people, but identifying with their experience on such a pro-

---

[2] *The New Dictionary of Catholic Spirituality* (Collegeville, MN: The Liturgical Press, 1993), s.v. "Compassion," by Michael Downey.

[3] Ibid.

[4] Ibid.

found level of one's being that one is moved to alleviate their pain and even share in their suffering. I am reminded of Elie Wiesel's description of a young boy who was hanged in the Buchenwald concentration camp during World War II before hundreds of fellow prisoners, all of whom who were forced to walk past him and look at him at close range. Once the chair was kicked out from under his legs, it took more than half an hour for him to die. As the boy was writhing in pain and bordering on death, someone asked, "Where is the merciful God, where is He?... For God's sake, where is God?" Wiesel's response captures the meaning of compassion: "And from within me, I heard a voice answer: Where is He? This is where—hanging from this gallows..."[5] The boy's suffering was God's suffering. In Wiesel's experience, the two had become intimately one.

For Christians, Jesus represents the fullness of compassion. As Emmanuel, "God with us" (Mt 1:23), he reveals to us through his life and ministry the compassion of God, whom he called "Ab-

---

[5] Elie Wiesel, *Night*, trans. Marion Wiesel (New York: Hill and Wang, 2006), 64-65.

ba, Father" (Rom 8:15). The Gospels are full of examples of his compassionate love for humanity: "In the New Testament, Jesus exemplifies God's compassion in his preaching and healing (Mt 9:6; 14:4), in his concern for lost humanity (Lk 19:41), and in his sacrificial love on the cross (Rom 5:8)."[6] What is more, the Scriptures tell us that "[t]he followers of Jesus are to live lives of compassion as an expression of the love that Jesus enjoined (Mt 5:4-7; Jn 13:34; Jas 2:8-18; 1 Jn 3:18)."[7] In the Gospels, moreover, "Jesus provided paradigms of compassion in the parables of the good Samaritan, who had compassion on the wounded traveler (Lk 10:33), and the prodigal son, whose father saw him in the distance and, 'moved with compassion,' ran to meet him (Lk 15:20)."[8]

Jesus' compassion stemmed from his relationship with his Father in heaven. He wanted that relationship to be the paradigm for all human relationships. In a world overwhelmed by sin and

---

[6] *The New Dictionary of Catholic Spirituality*, s.v. "Compassion," by Michael Downey.

[7] Ibid.

[8] Ibid.

suffering, however, he understood that the only
way to achieve this end would be not merely to
empathize with the suffering of others, but to embrace it as his own. He knew that an authentic and
true compassion for humanity would ultimately
lead to his own passion and death. Compassion, in
other words, ultimately manifests itself in passion.

One author who has seen the intrinsic link between Jesus' compassion and passion is the Jesuit
theologian, John Navone. In his book *Gospel Love:
A Narrative Theology*, he outlines "the link between the compassion of Jesus and his passion."[9]
He writes:

> The compassion of Jesus or his "suffering
> with" reaches its culmination in his passion,
> his "suffering for." In his compassion he
> moved to his passion, which John portrays as
> his loving "unto the end" (13:1). The compas-
> sion of Jesus becomes his passion as the final
> and ultimate sign of his being-in-Love. The
> passion is the culmination, or final moment,

---

[9] John Navone, *Gospel Love: A Narrative Theology*
(Wilmington, DE: Michael Glazier, 1984), 107.

of his compassion. The sign of the kingdom's coming is realized when compassion with others leads to passion for others: "A man can have no greater love than to lay down his life for his friends" (Jn 15:13). Compassion must become passion for the disciple as well as for the master, for this is the ultimate measure of our being-in-Love, in the Spirit that is the life of mutual indwelling of Father and Son.[10]

By entering the fullness of human suffering, by not only "suffering *with* us," but by also "suffering *for* us," Jesus established a new bond between humanity and divinity. Jesus, the God-man, who suffered and died for humanity, has gathered all of humanity into himself and paid the awful price for humanity's tragic flaw, the primordial desire to become God without God, to be Creator rather than creature, to make ourselves the center of the universe rather than the One from whom our origin stems. Jesus' passion and death, the ultimate expression of God's compassion for humanity, overcame the sin of human origins and put us

---

[10] Ibid., 107-8.

back in right relationship with the Father as his adopted sons and daughters. Jesus' solidarity with humanity, his desire "to suffer with" and "for us" was an integral part of his identity. He sacrificed himself on our behalf, that is, he made us holy (*sacrum facere*), so that we might enjoy life with him in the presence of the Father. Even now, he intercedes for us and mediates the grace of the Holy Spirit to us all because of the love he shares with the Father. The compassion of the Father manifests itself in the compassion and passion of Christ. The same holds true for his followers.

A wonderful example of someone who not only "suffered with," but also "suffered for" others was Maximilian Kolbe, a Conventual Franciscan who as a prisoner of war at Auschwitz volunteered to die for one of his inmates: "I am a Polish Catholic priest," he said. "I am old. I want to take this man's place because he has a wife and children." Kolbe was asked to step out of the line and was led into a starvation block and left to die.[11]

---

[11] Bert Ghezzi, *Voices of the Saints: A Year of Readings* New York: Doubleday, 2000), 520.

Here was someone whose compassion for another led him to make the ultimate sacrifice.

From Passion to Forgiveness

Jesus' compassion reaches its fullness in his passion, one of the major effects of which is his intercessory prayer from the cross, "Father, forgive them; for they do not know what they are doing" (Lk 23:34). Early on in his public ministry, he taught his followers to love their enemies and to pray for their persecutors (cf. Mt 5:44). His words from the cross demonstrate that he lived what he taught—even in death.

For most of us, forgiving someone who has hurt us is very difficult. It usually involves a long, drawn-out process of claiming the hurt, overcoming guilt for whatever role we might have had in causing it, finally recognizing that we have been victimized, reacting to it in righteous anger, and then moving to wholeness and mutual acceptance.[12] When asked how many times we

---

[12] See William A. Meninger, *The Process of Forgiveness* (New York: Continuum, 1997), 48-72.

should forgive our neighbors, Jesus responded not
seven times, but seventy times seven times (Mt
18:22). This startling response demonstrates how
central the act of forgiveness was to Jesus' life and
mission.

Although not easy to achieve, forgiving becomes less difficult over time. The more we forgive those who have hurt us, the less effort it requires. If we make it a priority in our lives, we
gradually find that a deeply rooted attitude has
grown within us, one that enables us to face life
and all that happens to us with a gentle, forgiving
heart. Such an attitude comes not through human
effort alone, but in conjunction with God's grace.
True forgiveness is a sign of God's presence in our
midst. It is a gift from the Lord, one for which all
of us should be deeply grateful.

Jesus possessed such a gentle, forgiving heart.
His entire life was about healing and forgiving. It
came easy for him because he did it so often and
because of his deep, intimate union with the Father. When he asks his Father to forgive his tormentors, he does so from a heart that, within a
short while, would be pierced by the lance of one

of the very men he is forgiving. By asking his Father to forgive, he teaches us that to hurt another person deliberately and unjustly is also a sin against God himself. As a result, the person who hurts another in this way ultimately hurts himself or herself in the process. This self-inflicted wound is what Jesus sees when he looks down from the cross and gazes upon his tormentors. Moved with compassion for them, he turns to his Father in heaven and intercedes on their behalf. He does the same for us whenever we injure ourselves in this way. Through his death, he takes our sins upon himself and pleads our cause. He is also asking his Father in heaven to forgive all of humanity. For this reason, his death on the cross was a key moment in the history of salvation. It was a primary means by which death lost its stranglehold over humanity.

Today's disciples must be, first and foremost, men and women of compassion: they "suffer with" others; they "suffer for" others; they forgive others, because they themselves have experienced the wonder and grace of God's merciful love. As the Pontifical Biblical Commission reminds us in,

The Bible and Morality: Biblical Roots of Christian Conduct, "[d]isciples who strive to imitate Jesus are told to adopt a way of life that now reflects the future reality of the kingdom; they must show compassion, not respond to violence, avoid sexual exploitation, take the initiative in reconciliation and love their enemies. Such dispositions... characterize the new life in the kingdom of God. Of these, reconciliation, pardon and unconditional love are central."[13]

Towards a Spirituality of Compassion

But just what does this mean in the concrete activities of our daily lives? What practical suggestions can we make for those of us who desperately seek to narrow the gap, who recognize the importance of living for Christ, yet who recognize in our own lives the vast distance between the ideal and the real, between the kind of people we desire to be and the kind of people we really are? How do we narrow the gap, especially when we have

[13] Pontifical Biblical Commission, *The Bible and Morality*, 141.

tried and tried so much in our spiritual lives and, in the end, feel, for whatever reasons, that we have fallen short? There are no easy answers to such difficult and probing questions. If spirituality, as Ronald Rolheiser suggests, is "what we do with the fire within us,"[14] then all we can do is to try to identify that fire and offer some concrete suggestions for how today's disciples can harness it in a constructive and truly compassionate way so they can lessen the gap in their experience between the ideal and the real with each new day. The five that follow are not exhaustive and are merely intended to point in the right direction.

To begin with, today's disciples must humbly acknowledge their shortcomings by means of a daily examen and regular sacramental confession. It is important for us to acknowledge where we are in our relationship with the Lord and where we would like to be. The Gospels remind us again and again that Jesus' earliest followers were weak, vulnerable men and women, who were full of imper-

---

[14] Ronald Rolheiser, *The Holy Longing: The Search for A Christian Spirituality* (New York: Doubleday, 1999), 11.

fections and human foibles, some of which were
quite visible—like Peter's brashness, Thomas's
doubting, James and John's bickering— and others of which were hidden in the dark places within
them and would come out only in moments of
crisis and deep peril. After all, they all ran away
and left him to face his enemies all alone. In one
way or another, they all denied him and, on some
level, even betrayed him, and it is important for us
to remember that we too have done the same at
various moments in our lives. As followers of Jesus, we are called to serve. It is important for us to
remember that there are times in our own lives
when we too may simply want to wash their hands
of everything and walk away. The apostles did it.
The question before us is how we will react to our
human shortcomings. Will we deny them, bury
them deep inside, project them on to others,
numb the pain they cause by anesthetizing themselves with drugs or alcohol? If we are not careful,
the burdens of our weaknesses, human shortcomings, and sinfulness will take their toll. To be men
and women of compassion and men and women
of forgiveness, we first need to take a good hard

look at ourselves and acknowledge where we are in their relationship with the Lord. We need to admit our faults to ourselves, to those we have hurt, and especially to God. We must humbly acknowledge how we ourselves have fallen short and missed the mark.

Today's disciples must foster their relationship with God through intimate and heartfelt prayer. In addition to acknowledging their faults and failings, today's disciples must recognize their need for God's help to overcome them. They need to humble themselves before the Lord, open their hearts to him, and place all their worries, concerns, sins, and moral imperfections, and spiritual wants in his hands. They need to take responsibility for their actions and seek forgiveness not only for their actions, but also for the deeply rooted attitudes of self-centeredness that lie behind so many of them. Sharing with the Lord from the heart is a fundamental prerequisite for anyone wishing to have an intimate relationship with him. Spiritual writers tell us that intimacy results from a combination of self-disclosure and loving atten-

tion.[15] If this is so, then to be intimate with the
Lord means that disciples are willing to share everything about themselves with him, as one friend
to another, and to spend time with him in prayer,
and especially before his presence in the Blessed
Sacrament. Today's disciples cannot be true men
and women of compassion if they do not have an
intimate friendship with Christ. They cannot an-
nounce Christ's message of love if they are not
deeply touched by a personal knowledge of that
love. They cannot forgive others if they themselves have never experienced forgiveness. It was
Jesus' intimate relationship with the Father which
led him to suffer *with* others, suffer *for* others, and
ask forgiveness for the sins of humanity while
hanging from the cross.

*Today's disciples must cultivate intimate
friendships and supports that will allow them to
share burdens with others and receive honest feed-
back about the appropriateness of their actions and
decisions.* Besides acknowledging their failings and

---

[15] See, for example, Pat Collins, *Intimacy and the
Hungers of the Heart* (Dublin/Mystic, CT: The Colum-
ba Press/Twenty-Third Publications, 1991), 142.

turning to God for help, disciples must not be afraid to allow their weaknesses and vulnerability to show. The Apostle Paul once wrote that it was when he was weak that he was strong (2 Cor 12:10). By this he meant that he was not relying on his own strength, but on the power of God working through his human weakness. The power of the Gospel shines through those who acknowledge their faults and trust in the Lord's saving grace. Being human, we all can easily be masters of self-deception, convincing ourselves, perhaps not in our minds, but possibly in our hearts, that we are building the kingdom primarily through our own efforts and that Jesus is only a secondary figure in our ordinary day-to-day affairs. If we manage to convince ourselves of this, then we will often try to hide our weaknesses, wear a disguise if you will. On the contrary, we need to allow God to be God in our lives and, in doing so, allow ourselves to be ourselves, and allow others to see us for who we truly are. We need to be authentic, genuine, and sincere. We need to be humble. "To be humble is to walk in truth," we are told.[16] People can always

---

[16] Teresa of Avila, *Interior Castle*, 6.10, trans. E. Al-

spot a fake, someone who, like the Pharisees criticized by Jesus in the Gospels, were more concerned with external appearances than the purity of their hearts. I am not saying that we need to wear our emotions on our sleeves but that we need to be comfortable in our own skins and should not be afraid to be with those we serve and share the Gospel with them from their hearts. We should be able to witness to others of how the power of the Gospel has touched our own lives. We need to be what the late Henri J. M. Nouwen called "wounded healers."[17] By inviting others into our own lives in this way, they will be more and more willing to allow us to enter their own. Only then will we be able to suffer with them. Only then will we be able to be men and women of compassion and forgiveness.

We need to cultivate the contemplative capacity to recognize the invisible presence of Christ in our midst in everything we do. We should be first and

---

lison Peers, Commentary by Dennis Billy (Notre Dame, IN: Christian Classics, 2007), 248.

[17] See Henri J. M. Nouwen, *The Wounded Healer: Ministry in Contemporary Society* (Garden City, NY: Doubleday, 1972).

foremost bearers of Christ to others. We are to live in deep personal communion and friendship with Christ and be so closely identified with him that the narrative of his life and ministry and of his passion, death and resurrection has become our own. When we encounter others, we carry this deep personal friendship with Christ with us, and we use the narrative of Christ's paschal mystery as the interpretative filter through which we make sense out of all that happens to us and to those we serve. As a result, we should mediate the presence of Christ to others and be a constant reminder to them that love, not chaos, lies at the root of all existence. Because we are men and women of faith and because of our close personal union with Christ, we also call upon others to delve beneath the level of appearances, deepen their faith, and encounter the person of Christ in their own lives. As friends of Christ, we carry his Spirit within our hearts wherever we go and can share that Spirit with everyone we meet. We are called "to live the Gospel on a deep level of consciousness" so that those we serve might do the same.[18] We see themselves as disciples of Christ and wish to follow him not on a part-time basis, or whenever it is convenient for us, but at every moment of their lives. We understand that they are *forever* followers of "the Way" and that *forever* begins in the *here and now.* Whenever Christ reigns in our hearts, whenever the desire to follow him is foremost, whenever he allows the Spirit to express himself through our own weaknesses and vulnerabilities, then it will be easy for us to be disciples who reach out and are able not only to suffer with but also suffer for others. We will find it easier to forgive ourselves for our own failings before God, to seek forgiveness for our sins, to forgive those who have hurt us, and to extend that forgiveness to others.

Finally, today's disciples must become experts in the art of forgiveness. As men and women of compassion, we must strive to become masters of the art of forgiveness. We understand that for-

---

[18] For the phrase "living the Gospel at a deep level of consciousness," see William Johnston, *Mystical Theology: The Science of Love* (London: HarperCollins, 1995), 9.

giveness was proclaimed by Jesus as a sign of God's presence in our midst. Just as Jesus forgave the sins of the paralytic, he now forgives all who come to them paralyzed by sinful habits and who have done actions that have been harmful to others and to their own souls. We understand that forgiveness involves a deep personal encounter with the Lord and that the Lord has chosen us to stand in a privileged place to see the deep spiritual wounds of those they serve and to reach out to them with words of healing and consolation. We see ourselves as those who both heal and who receive healing. We are humbled by the enormous trust that others place in us, and we do our best to step out of the way so that the Lord can work through us "to bring glad tidings to the poor, to proclaim liberty to captives, recovery of sight to the blind and release to prisoners" (Lk 4:18; see also Is 61:1). Forgiveness, for today's disciples, is the love of Christ made manifest in the lives of believers in a concrete way. We proclaim forgiveness, because we are men and women of compassion, because we are followers of the Way, because we are rooted in the love of Christ. We "suffer with" those who are haunted by their sins and encourage them to be reconciled with God and his Church. Through our prayers and actions, we witness the healing of souls and the renewal of relationships with God, with others, and with the self as we remember how Jesus acted toward those who came to him: "Has no one condemned you?" "Your sins are forgiven." "You may go. But from now on, avoid this sin" (Jn 8:10-11; Lk 5:23).

Conclusion

At the end of this reflection on compassion, I would like to return to Jesus' parable of the Good Samaritan and to a spiritual interpretation of it that comes from the Church fathers. In contrast to the priest and Levite, who as we saw in my opening remarks are the examples par excellence of men miserably lacking in compassion, authors such as Irenaeus of Lyons, Clement of Alexandria, Origen, Ambrose, Augustine, and John Chrysostom associate the Good Samaritan with Christ; the dying man, with fallen humanity; the oil, wine and dressing of the dying man's wounds, with the sacraments; the inn, with the Church; the innkeeper, with the apostles and their successors; and the eventual return of the Good Samaritan with Christ's second coming.[19]

The parable, according to this interpretation, reminds us that humanity's healing was made possible by Christ's compassionate love and continues to this day in the loving care Church. According to this interpretation of the parable, today's disciples are called to be men and of compassion, because Christ himself was a man of compassion. If we are lacking in this basic Christian quality, then something has gone terribly wrong with our understanding of discipleship. If we cannot "suffer with" others, how will we ever hope to follow in Christ's footsteps and "suffer for" them? A disciple without compassion is a

---

[19] See, for example, Origen, Homily 34.3, in *Origen: Homilies on Luke, Fragments on Luke*, trans., Joseph T. Lienhard (Washington, DC: Catholic University of America press, 1996), 138. See also New World Encyclopedia contributors, "Parable of the Good Samaritan," *New World Encyclopedia,* available online at http://www.newworldencyclopedia.org/entry/Parable_ of_the_Good_Samaritan?oldid=771732.

contradiction in terms. Such a person is not living the Gospel on a deep level of consciousness—and possibly not at all. Like the priest and Levite in the parable, he has seriously misunderstood the nature of his duties to God, to his neighbors, and ultimately to himself.

Most of us would agree that we have compassion and yet also in some way lacking in it. We strive to follow Jesus' example, but all too often find that the priest and Levite of the parable are still very much alive in us. Most of us recognize that there is a gap between the people of compassion we want to be and our lived experience. The question we must ask ourselves is whether that gap between vision and reality is getting larger or smaller. Or to put it another way, we must ask ourselves how often have we stopped to help someone in need as they make their way on the road Jerusalem to Jericho? How often have we turned a corner in time and stumbled upon a person in need without ever lifting a finger to help or, worse yet, meeting their eyes with a stare of cold indifference? Is the number of times getting increasing or decreasing?

In closing, let us pray that they may always be able to pray from the heart with the words of the Apostle Paul: "Praised be God, the Father of our Lord Jesus Christ, the Father of mercies, and the God of all consolation! He comforts us in all our afflictions and thus enables us to comfort those who are in trouble with the same consolation we have received from him" (2 Cor 1:3-4). And again, "I find my joy in the suffering I endure for you. In my own flesh I fill up what is lacking in the sufferings of Christ for the sake of his body, the church…. For this I work and struggle, impelled by that energy of his which is so powerful a force within me" (Col 1:24, 29).

The Blessings of the Beatitudes

- What is Mercy like?
- What does it consist of?
- Have you ever received it?
- Have you ever given it?
- Where does Mercy come from?
- From you or from God?

Prayer

Lord, you are all powerful, yet also all merciful. Look kindly upon your servant, or at least the servant I try to be. Have mercy on me! I am a sinner and know that I have no right whatsoever to be in your presence. Please help me to receive your mercy and forgiveness for my many sins and help me to extend that forgiveness to others in the way I live my life. I love you, Lord. Help me to love you more.

Chapter Six

Blessed are the Pure in Heart

"Blessed are the pure in heart, for they will see God" (Mt 5: 8). The story is told of a preacher who once put this question to a group of small children: "If all the good people were white and all the bad people were black, what color would you be?" One little girl raised her hand and said, "I think I'd be streaky!"[1] From the mouths of babes often comes the most obvious yet inconvenient of truths. It is for no small reason that Jesus makes becoming like a little child one of the prerequisites for entrance into the kingdom of heaven (See Mk 10:15; Mt 19:14; Lk 18:16).

Peering into Each Other's Hearts

If we were only able to peer into each other's hearts and see what we were really like. I daresay we would most likely find that we are all very

---

[1] See Anthony de Mello, *The Song of the Bird* (Garden City, NY: Image Books, 1984), 129.

much a mixture of extremes. Our hearts are divided, fragmented, drawn in opposite directions. They are "streaky" as the little girl says, a "mixed bag" of good and evil. We yearn for the good yet are pulled apart by so many worldly distractions that we sometimes feel as though we are going through life without purpose or direction. And yet, that is precisely what we need and so desperately want.

This chapter concerns the deepest longing of the human heart: to see God face-to-face. More specifically, it is about one of the beatitudes from Matthew's Gospel, the sixth one to be precise, the one that is normally translated: "Blessed are the pure in heart, for they shall see God" (Mt 5:8), the first part of which I prefer to translate as "Blessed are the single-hearted." My reason for preferring "single-heartedness" stems from my conviction that the beatitude in question concerns not merely being unsullied by worldly cares and the desires of the flesh, but "singleness of purpose and loyalty to God." As one author puts it, such an understanding of the beatitude "is more basic than moral purity, for it deals with honesty and integrity in our entire being."[2] If we ever hope to see God face-to-face, then our hearts must be entirely focused on him and on implementing his plan for our lives.

What Does It Mean to Be "Single-Hearted?"

To better understand what it means to be single-hearted we would do well to examine the meaning of the word "heart" itself. We find it listed close to 1,000 times in the Scriptures in various texts and contexts. Although it sometimes refers to the physical organ, it is more often used metaphorically to refer to some other dimension of human existence. At times, it refers to a person's ability to know and to understand. At other times, it is closely connected with memory. At still other times, it is closely associated with feeling. It is also tied in with a person's capacity to love. The word often refers to the whole person, especially when acting out of one's deepest, innermost core. From this point of view, "heart" refers to a per-

---

[2] *The New Catholic Dictionary of Spirituality* (1993), s.v. "Beatitude(s)," by Helen Doohan.

son's innermost self.[3] According to the editors of
The Philokalia, an anthology of Eastern Christian
spiritual teachings from the fourth through fif-
teenth centuries, the heart is

> "…not simply the physical organ but the spir-
> itual center of man's being, man as made in
> the image of God, his deepest and truest self,
> or the inner shrine, to be entered only through
> sacrifice and death in which the mystery of the
> union between the divine and human is con-
> summated. 'I called with my whole heart,' says
> the psalmist—that is, with body, soul and spir-
> it…. 'Heart' has thus an all-embracing signifi-
> cance: 'prayer of the heart' means prayer not
> just of the emotions and affections, but of the
> whole person, including the body."[4]

---

[3] For an extended treatment of these themes, see
Andrew Tessarolo, "Symbolic Christian Significance of
the Word 'Heart:' A Biblical Approach." Available on
the website of the Congregation of the Priests of the
Sacred Heart, http://www.netsonic.fi/~scjregfi.

[4] *The Philokalia: The Complete Text*, trans. and
eds. G.E.H. Palmer, Philip Sherrard, Kallistos Ware,
vol. 4 (London: Faber and Faber, 1995), 431.

Today, when Christians speak of "heart," they would do well to use it in this all-embracing, comprehensive sense.

Closely related to "heart," although narrower and perhaps even more fundamental in scope, is the concept of "conscience," which is associated with practical reason and exhorts a person to do good and avoid evil. In *Veritatis splendor*, his encyclical on fundamental questions of the Church's moral teaching, the late Pope John Paul II emphasizes the close relationship between the two. "The relationship between man's freedom and God's law," he says, "is most deeply lived out in the 'heart' of the person, in his moral conscience."[5] He then quotes from *Gaudium et spes*, no. 16 to demonstrate the important role played by conscience in safeguarding human dignity and determining man's destiny: "Always summoning him to love good and avoid evil, the voice of conscience can when necessary speak to his heart more specifically: 'do this, shun that.' For man has in his heart a law written by God. To obey it is the

---

[5] John Paul II, *Veritatis splendor*, no. 54 (Vatican City: Libreria Editrice Vaticana, 1993), 85.

very dignity of man; according to it he will be judged."[6]

Theologians today typically refer to conscience in terms of capacity, process, and judgment. Human beings have the *capacity* to discern good from evil, do so through a *process* of deliberation, and make concrete *judgments* about what action to take.[7] Taken as a whole, conscience is "the most intimate center and sanctuary of a person."[8] When properly formed, it "guarantees freedom and engenders peace of heart."[9] Conscience enables us to listen to the law inscribed in our hearts by God so that we can appropriately discern right from wrong. To act from the heart

---

[6] Ibid. See also Second Vatican Council, *Gaudium et spes*, no. 16 in *Decrees of the Ecumenical Councils*, 2: 1077.

[7] For a listing of some of the better-known theological presentations of conscience, see Dennis J. Billy and James F. Keating, *Conscience and Prayer: The Spirit of Catholic Moral Theology* (Collegeville, Minn.: The Liturgical Press, 2001), 12n.22.

[8] Second Vatican Council, *Gaudium et spes*, no. 16 in *Decrees of the Ecumenical Councils*, 2: 1077.

[9] *Catechism of the Catholic Church*, par. 1784 (Vatican City: Libreria Editrice Vaticana, 1994), 440.

means to act according to one's conscience and to be involved totally in that action, on every dimension of one's being: the physical, emotional, intellectual, spiritual, and social. To be pure and single of heart, therefore, is to be someone totally committed to truth and passionately involved in living one's life in close communion with God.

A Look at the Sports World

I think we can find a fitting analogy for what it means to be single-hearted in the world of sports. One of the things we admire most about our sports heroes is their capacity to stay focused under intense pressure for extended periods of time. Whether it be Tiger Woods putting on the eighteenth green to clutch yet another PGA tournament, or Roger Federer netting yet another Grand Slam title, or Michael Phelps splashing his way a record eight gold medals in Olympic swimming, or Jamaican sprinter Usain Bolt smashing the world record in the 100 meter dash once again, we stand in awe of their capacity to overcome physical adversity and the opposing demons of self-doubt and cocky, over-confidence to rise to the occasion and sustain one stellar performance after another in the midst of difficult odds and stiff competition.

Such athletes compete as much against themselves as they do against others. They keep their eyes on the prize over the long haul and reap the fruits of a disciplined regimen of physical and mental training that puts them at the top of their game and gives them an edge against their competitors. They give their hearts to the goal before them and are willing to face impossible odds to achieve it. We admire these heroes, and a part of us wants to be like them. What makes them stand out is their single-hearted devotion to being the very best in their field. They have focused on a goal and dedicated themselves entirely to achieving it. We are inspired by their athletic pursuits and would like to do something similar in our lives that we could be proud of.

Although what I have said about our sports heroes can just as easily be applied to any field of human endeavor— be it teaching, writing, medicine, or what have you—the reason why I chose an analogy from sports to introduce my topic is because the Apostle Paul uses it to make a similar point about the spiritual life. In his First Letter to the Corinthians, he likens the Christian life to running a race: "Do you not know that in a race the runners all compete, but only one receives the prize? Run in such a way that you may win it. Athletes exercise self-control in all things; they do it to receive a perishable wreath, but we an imperishable one" (1 Cor 9:24-25). In his Letter to the Philippians, he employs the same analogy when referring to himself: "I press on toward the goal for the prize of the heavenly call of God in Christ Jesus" (Phil 3:14).

For Paul, the life of Christian discipleship means having single-hearted devotion to winning the imperishable crown of everlasting life. Like the runners in a race, we must deny ourselves many things to achieve this goal. Unlike all the runners in a race, however, it is possible for *each of us* to win. This is what the good news of Jesus Christ is all about. Paul was aware, however, that even the most devoted runners can stumble and fall. He was conscious aware of his own weaknesses and shortcomings and averts to them at various points in his letters (see, for example, Rom 7:14-25; 2 Cor 12:7-10; 1 Tm 1:15). Still, when all is said and done, he firmly believed that because of Jesus' passion, death, and resurrection, each of us can hope one day of seeing God face-to-face. All that is necessary is for us to open our hearts, our minds, our consciences, to him and allow him to help us and gently transform us so that we can do the one thing necessary—to love and follow him all the days of our lives—with greater and greater ease.

The Rich Young Man

In stark contrast to Paul's total and unflinching dedication to Christ and the call of Christian discipleship is the story of the rich young man of Matthew's Gospel (see Mt 19: 16-22). Jesus has just finished telling his disciples that they must become like little children to enter the kingdom of heaven. Moved by these words a young man approaches Jesus and asks him what he must do to gain eternal life. Jesus tells him to keep the commandments and goes on to cite many of those listed in the Decalogue: "You shall not murder; You shall not commit adultery; You shall not steal; You shall not bring false witness. Honor your father and mother; also, You shall love your neighbor as yourself" (Mt 19: 18-19). The young man tells Jesus that he has kept these commandments and wants to know what more he must do. Jesus looks at the young man and tells him that if he wants to be perfect he must sell all that he owns, give the money to the poor, and then follow him. Hearing these words, the young man goes away sad, for he is a man of great wealth.

This rich young man represents the epitome of someone with a restless, divided heart. He yearns for everlasting life but is not willing to place his complete trust in God. He keeps the commandments but cannot bring himself to let go of his many possessions, the very things that weigh him down and prevent him from following the way of the Lord Jesus with his whole heart, mind, soul, and strength. He finds himself pulled in two directions: toward God and toward his many possessions. He walks away sad because he cannot bring himself to do the one thing now being asked of him. Jesus then turns to his disciples and warns them of the danger of riches, saying that it is more difficult for a camel to pass through the eye of a needle than for a rich man to enter the kingdom of heaven (see Mt 19:23-24).

In many ways, the story of the rich young man is our own. We too often find ourselves pulled in two directions. We too yearn for eternal life yet find it difficult to let go of the very things that hinder us from achieving it. We too feel burdened by the things of this world yet are afraid to let go and place our complete trust in God. It remains to be seen just what we will do. Will we follow the way of the Lord Jesus or walk away sad? The choice is before us and the outcome rests on our shoulders.

Have you ever wondered why so many people in this world suffer from depression? I understand that this is a complex question, and I do not wish to call into question any of the underlying medical and psychological causes of the condition. I cannot help but feel, however, that it may also be an underlying spiritual reason for it. Could it not be that at least part of the reason why so many of us suffer from a constant, throbbing, and gnawing sense of emptiness inside of ourselves is because somewhere along the line we have lost touch with the only thing that will make us truly happy? Could it be that we have misplaced the true allegiance of our hearts in exchange for false substitutes that can in no way fill our deepest yearnings for happiness and transcendence? It was St. Augustine who said, "[Lord], you have made us for yourself and our hearts are restless until they can find peace in you."[10] I sometimes wonder if the melancholy and deep sense of sadness that pervades the lives of so many people in this world (and, at times, possibly our own) is to due misplaced affections, unrealistic hopes, and a failure to recognize that, in the end, only God can truly satisfy the unquiet and restless longings of the human heart. Rather than emulating the Apostle Paul by focusing our entire attention on the finish line and running toward the prize to which God has called us, we follow instead the example of the rich young man, who turned from Jesus and walked away sad. I sometimes wonder if at least a

---

[10] Augustine of Hippo, *Confessions*, 1.1.

partial cause of depression is our refusal to let go
of the things we think will make us happy, but
which ultimately do nothing but get in the way of
our ongoing transformation in Christ. Generally
good in themselves and most likely different for
each person, these things, whatever they may be—
wealth, power, fame, pleasure—eventually lose
their glitter and fail to satisfy. Instead of making
us happy, they weigh us down and, if we are not
careful, can obtain extraordinary power over us.
Our possessions, in other words, can take posses-
sion of us. Instead of freeing us, they weigh us
down and eventually enslave us. We ultimately
become them and, in so doing, lose our souls. This
is what C. S. Lewis calls the "abolition of man,"
which comes from focusing our heart's deepest
desire on the things that will ultimately enslave us
rather than on the one "thing" that will make us
free and truly happy.[11]

It would be a mistake for us to think, however,
that the healing of a divided heart can take place
in a single instant or that happiness comes about

---

[11] C. S. Lewis, *The Abolition of Man* (New York:
Macmillan, 1947; tenth printing, 1973), 83-84.

by letting go of our material possessions in one fell swoop. When we unburden ourselves of the things that weigh us down, these very things continue have a subtle, invisible hold over us. While it is true that all things are possible for God, it seems that most of us spend our entire lives struggling against these opposing internal forces. This holds true even for those who have entered the priesthood and religious life and who have publicly professed to live a dedicated life of Christian discipleship. The story is told in the traditions of Eastern Orthodoxy of a certain Abba Moses, a desert father who instructed his disciples on purity of heart with these words:

> We give up country, family, possessions, and everything worldly in order to acquire purity of heart. If we forget this purpose we cannot avoid frequently stumbling and losing our way, for we will be walking in the dark and straying from the proper path. This has happened to many men who at the start of their ascetic life gave up all wealth, possessions, and everything worldly, but who later flew into a

rage over a fork, a needle, a rush or a book. This would not have happened to them had they borne in mind the purpose for which they gave up everything.[12]

What are the things in life that can easily throw you in a rage? They may not be as simple and unimportant as a needle or a fork, but Abba Moses' words challenge us to examine our hearts and identify those small and seemingly insignificant things that still have power over us and have caused us to compromise the primary allegiance of our hearts. He reminds us that there are other things beside material possessions that can gain power over and enslave the soul. In the Christian tradition they are known as the Seven Deadly Sins—and Anger is one of them. The other six are: Pride, Covetousness, Lust, Gluttony, Envy, and Sloth. I sometimes wonder if we are fully aware of how easily we can deceive ourselves and fall under the sway of these powerful internal forces. By focusing on small, petty, seemingly insignificant, almost invisible objects of desire (e.g., small ex-

---

[12] *The Philokalia*, 1:95-96.

pressions in everyday life of one's wealth, power, and importance) these vices can become deeply rooted in us and influence our behavior in ways in which we are not even fully conscious. Abba Moses reminds us that to be pure and single of heart we must also confront our wild and unruly passions and cooperate with the movements of God's grace in our lives to that they will be tamed by the gentle sway of reason's rule. Only then will we be free to follow God's will for our lives. Only then will we be able to enter the kingdom of heaven. Only then will we be able to see God face-to-face. To put it another way, we must train our souls rigorously so that the image of God in us can be polished and light of God's grace allowed to shine in us ever more brightly and transform us into the sons and daughters he originally intended us to be. This can happen only to the single-hearted. It is the primary requirement for all those who desire entrance into the kingdom of heaven. It alone will enable them to keep their sights fixed on their final destination.

It is also important for us to remember that this kind of purity of heart is first and foremost a work of God and is made possible through the action of his grace. The second-century Church father Irenaeus of Lyons (c. 180) affirms this in his commentary on purity and singleness of heart when he says: "It is true, because of the greatness and inexpressible glory of God, that 'man shall not see me and live,' for the Father cannot be grasped. But because of God's love and goodness toward us, and because he can do all things, he goes so far as to grant those who love him the privilege of seeing him…. For 'what is impossible for men is possible for God.'"[13] The vision of God, in his mind, is a gift of God given only to those who truly love him. In this respect, the pure and single-hearted love God so much that God has decided to unite their hearts with his. Purity of heart, in other words, is a total gift from God and cannot be achieved by human effort alone.

Centuries later, the author of the eighteenth-century spiritual classic *Abandonment to Divine Providence*, usually attributed to Jean-Pierre de

---

[13] *Catechism of the Catholic Church*, par. 1722, p. 428.

Caussade (1675-1751), also refers to the purity and singleness of heart in terms of gift:

> Let others, Lord, ask you for all sorts of gifts. Let them increase their prayers and entreaties. But I, my Lord, ask for one thing only and have only a single prayer—give me a pure heart! How happy we are if our hearts are pure! Through the ardor of our faith we see God as he is. We see him in everything and at every moment working within and around us. And in all things we are both his subject and his instrument. He guides us everywhere and leads us to everything. Very often we do not think about it, but he thinks for us. It is enough that we have desired what is happening to us and must happen to us by his will.[14]

Here, purity or singleness of heart is depicted as a gift from God that cleanses the soul of its inordinate passions and empowers it to see the hand

---

[14] Jean-Pierre de Caussade, *Abandonment to Divine Providence*, trans. John Beevers (Garden City, NY: Image Books, 1975), 68.

of God in all the circumstances of one's present life. The gift of self-abandonment helps us to find God in the duties and responsibilities of the present moment and readies us for the perfect vision that will come in the world to come. When seen in this light, purity or singleness of heart is that God-given quality of soul that enables us to join mystically in Christ's humble self-emptying, a process that helps us to forget ourselves and put the interest of others before our own.

A Twofold Gift

What sets pure and single-hearted persons apart? They love God with every fiber of their being. In return for their love, God blesses them with a twofold gift. First, his grace cleanses and purifies their passions so they are no longer distracted by the cares of this world or hindered by temptations that divide their affections and put in them a state of double mindedness. Secondly, God's grace strengthens their intellects through the gift of understanding and enables them see God imperfectly in this life, as a reflection in a mirror, and perfectly in the next by way of the beatific vision.

What do pure and single-hearted persons desire? They desire one thing and one thing only: to do God's will. They are willing to suffer and endure all things, even death itself, to achieve it. They do so not to make satisfaction for their sins, or to gain some temporal or even spiritual reward, but simply because they love God and desire to please him. They seek God in all things. They long to do his will and welcome whatever crosses come their way. They are patient amid adversity, persevering in their faithfulness, and steadfast in their desire to do God's will, the one thing that is necessary.

What are the signs of purity and singleness of heart? Single-hearted persons are not disturbed when their undertakings are unsuccessful. They rejoice at the good done by others, as if it were their own. They are not ambitious about the positions they are asked to fill. They do not seek praise or approval for their good works. They see God's will as it is manifested to them in the duties and responsibilities of the present moment. They believe that God is working at every moment both within them and in the world around them. They trust God above all else and believe that all things work out for the good.

Who is the model of the pure and single-hearted person? Our discourse now takes us back to the New Testament and the longstanding wisdom of Church tradition to find such a person in Mary, the mother of Jesus. "Hail Mary, full of grace! The Lord is with you."[15] These opening words of the "Hail Mary," words rooted in Scripture and one of the most treasured prayers of Catholic devotion, present the Blessed Mother as God's highly-favored daughter and the epitome of someone with an undivided heart, someone who wishes to do one thing and only one thing, indeed, the one thing necessary. "Let it be done unto me according to your will."[16] Her humble fiat reflects

---

[15] The traditional rendering of Lk 1:28 (the opening words of the *Hail Mary*). *The New Revised Standard Version* translates it, "Greetings, favored one! The Lord is with you."

[16] The traditional rendering of Lk 1:38. *The New Revised Standard Version* translates it, "Let it be with me according to your word."

her dogged desire to do God's will, even in the most difficult of circumstances. It reminds us that even though her heart was deeply troubled by the angel's words, she received them with joy and trusted that the Lord would do great things for her. "My soul proclaims the greatness of the Lord." She, more than anyone else, sought to carry out God's will in her life with every fiber of her being. These words reveal the great joy she found in doing the Lord's will, regardless of the deep grief and suffering it would cause her. "Blessed is the fruit of your womb, Jesus." She not only carried Jesus in her womb, but her heart was uniquely united to his. Her heart was one with his—and his with her. These words remind us that Mary brought Christ into the world and could do so only because her entire being—her mind, her soul, her very womb—was uniquely prepared by God to receive the seed of humanity's hope and ultimate transformation. Like Mary, God empties the hearts of the pure and single-hearted and fills them with his love. Like Mary, the pure and single-hearted are blessed because God has blessed them for their sincere desire to love and serve him. Like Mary, they see God because God peers into their hearts, opens his heart to them, and dwells within them. This mutual indwelling of hearts is a mark of friendship and a sure sign of purity and singleness of heart.[17]

Conclusion

What kind of a heart do you have? A pure heart? An evil heart? A streaky heart? Unless there are some verifiable saints in our midst, I daresay most of us would say streaky! I would also like to nuance the possible answers to this question by looking at the three New Testament figures whom we have examined over the course of this chapter—the rich young man, the Apostle Paul, and the Blessed Virgin Mary—and make a nuanced distinction that I do not believe has ever been made before.

I believe we need to widen the category of the sixth beatitude to include a variety of types of pu-

---

[17] The three marks of friendship are benevolence, reciprocity, and mutual indwelling. See Paul Wadell, *Friendship and the Moral Life*, 130-41.

rity and singleness of heart to better correspond to human experience. I would like to suggest three levels that correspond to the purgative, illuminative, and unitive ways.[18] For the purgative way, which primarily concerns beginners in the spiritual life, there is the restless, divided heart as in the case of the rich young man. For the illuminative way, which concerns those who have made progress in the spiritual life, there is the restless, undivided heart, as in the case of the Apostle Paul. For the unitive way, which concerns those who have crossed the finished line and won the imperishable crown of intimate friendship with God, there is the pure and single heart, as in the case of the Blessed Mother.

The question that should remain for us is not what kind of heart do you have? I think most of us already know the answer to that question. I think the real question is what kind of heart would you like to have? And closely following that one is the

---

[18] For the Scriptural and historical foundations of the Threefold Way, see *The New Catholic Dictionary of Spirituality* (Collegeville, MN: The Liturgical Press, 1993), s.v. "The Three Ways," by Thomas D. McGonigle.

question: Is your heart gradually becoming more and more divided, restless, and burdened by the worries and cares of the world or is it more and more focused on the finish line, on doing the one thing that matters, on winning the imperishable crown of everlasting life? Such questions need to be pondered deeply in the quiet of our hearts where we can be honest with ourselves before God and ask his help in doing the one thing that matters. "Blessed are the pure in heart, for they will see God" (Mt 5:8). When we look within our hearts, we may feel that such a possibility, to see God face-to-face, is difficult to imagine and perhaps even a bit presumptuous. We need to remember, however, Jesus' words to his disciples as he watched the rich young man walk away in sadness: "For God all things are possible" (Mt 19:26). Let us give God room to purify, illumine, and unify our hearts with his. Let us turn to him with open hearts and ask him to make them pure and singularly focused on doing the one thing necessary, that is, making the fiat of Mary and of Jesus our own, so that his kingdom may come, and his will may be done on earth as it is in heaven.

The Blessings of the Beatitudes

- What is purity of heart?
- What does it mean to focus on the one thing that matters?
- What gets in the way of your being single-hearted?
- Why is purity of heart a prerequisite for seeing God?
- Do you have a divided heart?
- Do you want your heart to be pure and clean?

Prayer

Lord, I look inside my heart and do not like what I see. Rather than seeing you, with a pure heart, I see so many conflicting earthly wants that get in the way of my relationship with you and pull me down. Cleanse my heart, Lord. Purify it. Make me whole. I want to see you. I long to see you! Yet all too often I get in the way of the movement of your Spirit in my life and prefer to go my own way. Help me, Lord. Help me! Help me to respond to the promptings of your Spirit. Deepen in me the longing to see you face-to-face. Purify my heart so that I may be whole.

Chapter Seven

Blessed Are the Peacemakers

"Blessed are the peacemakers, for they shall be called children of God" (Mt 5:9). In this chapter, we will explore how Jesus, the "Prince of Peace," ministers to our deep inner longings and show how the Church assists in this process when it opens its rich spiritual heritage and offers people the possibility of a profound personal encounter with him. It does so especially when it breathes with both lungs, that is, with the best its Eastern and Western traditions have to offer.[1] When we follow Jesus along the way of discipleship, he gives us peace of heart, molds us into becoming peacemakers like him, and sees us, his brothers and sisters, as the adopted sons and daughters of his Father.

---

[1] This theme was often emphasized by Pope John Paul II. See, for example, his reflection on his visit to Romania, *General Audience*, Wednesday, May 12, 1999, and his "Angelus," address on Friday, June 29, 2001.

Peace of Heart

The word, "heart" occurs close to 1,000 times in the Scriptures. Although it sometimes refers to the physical organ, it is more often used metaphorically to refer to some other dimension of human existence. At times, it refers to a person's ability to know and to understand. At other times, it is closely connected with memory. At still other times, it is closely associated with feeling. It is also associated with a person's capacity to love. As we saw in the last chapter, the word often refers to the whole person, especially when acting out of one's deepest, innermost core. From this point of view, "heart" refers to a person's innermost self.[2]

"Shalom," the Hebrew word for "peace," is the common Jewish way of extending a greeting or biding someone farewell. It is usually taken as an expressed hope for wholeness or completeness. It

---

[2] For an extended treatment of these themes, see Andrew Tessarolo, "Symbolic Christian Significance of the Word 'Heart:' A Biblical Approach." Available on the website of the Congregation of the Priests of the Sacred Heart at http://www.netsonic.fi/~scjregfi.

can be used in a variety of contexts: material, personal, relational, societal. To wish someone "shalom" is to desire his or her well-being. It is to wish that all things exist in harmony both within and around the person. "Peace" or "shalom" implies a desire for a person not only to be without injury, but also to experience wholeness within, in one's relations with others, and with God. Jesus extends his "peace" to his disciples several times in the Gospels. In John's Gospel, for example, he says, "'Peace' is my farewell to you, my peace if my gift to you; I do not give it to you as the world gives peace" (Jn 14:27). Here, Jesus is drawing upon a more profound meaning of the term. As Bruce Vawter points out:

> The word had a much deeper significance… as an expression of the harmony and communion with God that was the seal of the covenant (cf. Nm 6:26). Hence it came to have an eschatological and messianic meaning (cf. Is 9:6), virtually the same as salvation. It is this spiritual tranquility that Christ gives, which has no resemblance to what the world gives. Be-

cause Christ is this gift that he gives (Eph 2:14) can call him "our peace."[3]

St. Augustine of Hippo (354-430) draws upon the covenantal, eschatological, and messianic aspects of this Biblical notion when he defines peace as "tranquility of order." Although he provides no general or systematic presentation of the term, he gives it a primary place on every level of existence: the material, the irrational, the rational, the social, and the spiritual. His vision shines through in a much-celebrated passage from *The City of God*:

> The peace of the body... is a tempering of the component parts in duly ordered proportion, the peace of the irrational soul is a duly ordered repose of the appetites; the peace of the rational soul is the duly ordered agreement of cognition and action. The peace of the body and soul is the duly ordered life and health of

---

[3] Bruce Vawter, "The Gospel According to John," in *The Jerome Biblical Commentary*, eds. Raymond E. Brown, Joseph A. Fitzmyer, and Roland E. Murphy (Englewood Cliffs, N.J.: Prentice-Hall, 1968), 454.

a living creature; peace between mortal man and God is an ordered obedience, in faith, in subjection to an everlasting law; peace between men is an ordered agreement of mind with mind; the peace of a home is the ordered agreement among those who live together about giving and obeying orders; *the peace of the city is an ordered agreement of the citizens with respect to commanding and obeying*; the peace of the heavenly City is a perfectly ordered and perfectly harmonious fellowship in God; the peace of the whole universe is the tranquility of order—and order is the arrangement of things equal and unequal in a pattern which assigns to each its proper position.[4]

Augustine presents here an analogous vision of peace that embraces both the internal and external dimensions of human existence. The anthropological features of his understanding of peace are especially worth noting. Rather than simply incorporating into his presentation the

---

[4] Augustine of Hippo, *The City of God*, 19.13.

tendency towards dualism that haunts nearly all Platonic and Neoplatonic renderings of human existence, Augustine is emphatic in maintaining the intrinsic unity between the spiritual and the corporeal: "The peace of body and soul is the duly ordered life and health of a living creature." He is also able to emphasize the intrinsic social dimensions of human existence (e.g., *pax hominum, pax domus, pax civitatis*) and thereby escapes the marked tendency toward introversion that had, by Augustine's time, become so closely associated with the Neoplatonic tradition. This anthropological cohesiveness on the personal and social levels makes "peace" the dominant ideal of all Augustinian social thought. It is the *telos* toward which his massive body of ethical teaching moves. It bears noting, moreover, that the order of love and the order of justice parallel Augustine's "analogy of peace" at every level and converge at their teleological focus of the Supreme Good, where the tranquility of order exists as an absolute value. Since the present world suffers from the effects of original sin, however, no one can have a temporal experience of these orders that is not totally free of a least some element of perversion. For this reason, peace in this life—even "peace of heart" —is always imperfect. The appetites will never be fully tamed, nor will reason and will find rest in any earthly treasure. Augustine says it well in the opening lines of his *Confessions*, "O Lord… you have made us for yourself, and our hearts are restless until they find peace in you."[5]

Thomas Aquinas (1224/25-74) uses Augustine's definition of peace for his point of departure and, with the application of his honed scholastic dialectic, draws out many of its hidden implications. Although all of creation loves peace and strives for it, he believes that human beings pursue it as a fundamental value on three important levels: with the self, with others, and with God. The first involves a calming of one's inordinate passions and desires; the second, existing in right relationship with one's neighbor; the third, surrendering oneself totally to the will of God.[6] Because a person is capable of pursuing an apparent good rather than a real good, moreover, he also makes a

---

[5] Augustine of Hippo, *The Confessions*, 1.1.

[6] Aquinas, S*th.*, II-II, q. 29, a. 3, resp.

distinction between real and apparent peace.[7] Real peace, he believes, requires a calming of our desires and freedom from external disturbances.[8] Because these two conditions can never be fully realized in this world, perfect peace is unattainable in this life.[9] Even real peace, however imperfect in this life, is a gift of God. It comes from Christ, the "Prince of Peace," through his gift of the Spirit.[10] Through his Spirit, Christ imparts a peace that the world cannot give. This peace manifests itself in this life in a disdain for material wealth, in a calming of the passions, and in the contemplation of divine wisdom. In the future life, it manifests itself in the riches of eternal goods, freedom from all evil, and stability.[11] Peace, for Aquinas, is an effect of charity, a virtue that enables a person to love God with one's whole heart and to love one's neighbor as oneself.[12] Love unifies, and peace

---

[7] Ibid., II-II, q. 29, a. 2, ad 3m.

[8] Ibid., I-II, q. 70, a. 3, resp.

[9] Ibid., II-II, 29, a. 2, ad 4m.

[10] Ibid., I-II, q. 70, a. 1, resp.

[11] Thomas Aquinas, *Lectura super Iohannem*, c. 14, lect. 7.

[12] Aquinas, *Sth.*, II-II, q. 29, a. 3, resp.

flows from the union of appetites and the soul's inner powers.[13] Peace, for Aquinas, is not a virtue, but a beatitude and fruit of the Spirit. As a beatitude, it is one of the most perfect acts of charity and corresponds to the gift of wisdom, the gift of the Spirit most closely associated with charity.[14] Peace, after all, is the "tranquility of order," and it is for wisdom to set things in order.[15] As a fruit of the Spirit, it represents a final good that both contains within itself and conveys spiritual sweetness.[16]

Truth and Peace of Heart

From what we have seen thus far, we may say that peace of heart concerns the whole person but focuses especially on the interior life as the life-giving spring from which all else flows. It cannot be attained through human effort alone but must be received as a gift of God and of Christ, the

---

[13] Ibid., II-II, q. 29, a. 3, ad 3m.

[14] Ibid., II-II, q. 29, a. 4, resp. ; ad 3m.

[15] Ibid., II-II, q. 45, a. 6, resp.

[16] Ibid., II-II, q. 29, a. 4, ad 1m.

"Prince of Peace." Because of the effects of original sin, peace of heart will always be imperfect in this life and must look to the hereafter for its fulfillment. Fallen human nature has both bodily and spiritual wounds: those of the body are sensibility to suffering and mortality; those of the soul are ignorance, malice, lack of courage, and inordinate concupiscence.[17] When seen in this light, a person will never have full peace of heart so long as the external disturbances of death and physical pain pose a threat to one's life and as long as reason, will, and the irascible and concupiscible appetites remain in their weakened state. That said, it is important to remember that there are varying degrees of imperfection and that true peace of heart, even in its imperfect state, involves a gradual transformation of a person so that his or her life—in both its internal and external dimensions—is more and more ordered to a life lived in the Spirit. The "tranquility of order" that Christ, the "Prince of Peace" imparts through his Spirit to those will-

---

[17] See, for example, Ludwig Ott, *Fundamentals of Catholic Dogma*, trans. Patrick Lynch (Rockford, Ill.: Tan Books and Publishers, 1974), 113.

ing to receive it is the tranquility of his resurrected life. This new life, this first fruit of the new creation, can now take root in our own and effect in us a reordering of our lives from the inside out.

To my mind, one of the best descriptions of peace of heart comes from Gregory of Nyssa (c.335-c.395), often hailed as the father of Christian mysticism, in his treatise *On Christian Perfection*. I came across this passage quite unexpectedly as I was praying "The Office of Readings" as part of *The Liturgy of the Hours*, the universal prayer of the Church. The passage comes from the second reading for Thursday in the Nineteenth Week of Ordinary Time and reads:

> "He [Christ] is our peace, for he has made us both one." Since we think of Christ as our peace, we may call ourselves true Christians only if our lives express Christ by our own peace. As the Apostle says: "He has put enmity to death." We must never allow it to be rekindled in us in any way but must declare that it is absolutely dead. Gloriously has God slain enmity, in order to save us, may we never risk

the life of our souls by being resentful or by bearing grudges. We must not awaken that enmity or call it back to life by our wickedness, for it is better left dead.

No, since we possess Christ who is peace, we must put an end to this enmity and live as we believe he lived. He broke down the separating wall, uniting what was divided, bringing about peace by reconciling in his single person those who disagreed. In the same way, we must be reconciled not only with those who attack us from outside, but also with those who stir up dissension within; flesh then will no longer be opposed to the spirit, nor the spirit to the flesh. Once we subject the wisdom of the flesh to God's law, we shall be re-created as one single man at peace. Then, having become one instead of two, we shall have peace within ourselves.

Now peace is defined as harmony among those who are divided. When, therefore, we end that civil war within our nature and cultivate peace within ourselves, we become peace. By this peace we demonstrate that the name of

Christ, which we bear, is authentic and appropriate.[18]

Gregory's words, to my mind, give us a key insight into the relationship between "truth" and "peace of heart." True Christians are those whose lives express Christ through their own peace. We can do so, only if we "cultivate peace within ourselves" and allow that peace to flow through our actions. We cultivate this inner peace by ending the civil war within our nature so that our divided souls might be healed and made whole. We can do this only because, as Gregory says, Christ "has put enmity to death" and has himself become our peace. True peace of heart is a gradual process through which Christ's peace becomes our own. Only by allowing his peace to dwell within us and eventually permeate our hearts will we be worthy to bear his name. Only then will we be authentic followers, real disciples, true Christians. If truth, for a Christian, is the living God, then peace of

---

[18] Gregory of Nyssa, *On Christian Perfection* in *The Liturgy of the Hours*, vol. 4 (New York: Catholic Book Publishing, Co., 1975), 106-7.

heart comes about when a person enters a truthful relationship with him. To live in truth is to live in communion with Jesus, the source of truth and life. To live in truth is to live in friendship with the one who laid down his life for his friends. To live in truth is to make the way of the Lord Jesus our own. It is Christ's gift of the Spirit that makes this possible. The Spirit of Truth and of Life is also the Spirit of Peace.

Forming True Peace of Heart

Let us now turn to the question of how to nurture "the truth of peace" within a person's heart. Let us begin by saying that, to my mind, the deep interior spaces of the human heart may well be the most challenging mission territory facing the Church in this new millennium. The "dictatorship of relativism," as Benedict XVI so aptly calls it, has caused many in Western society to lose their bearings and sense of purpose in life.[19] These people

---

[19]As Dean of the Sacred College of Cardinals, Cardinal Joseph Ratzinger used the phrase, "the dictatorship of relativism" in a homily preached at the Votive

hunger for transcendence, but are trapped in a culture so blinded by the reductive forces of materialism and consumerism that it is very difficult for them to see that their hunger was meant to be satisfied and actually points to something beyond themselves. What is more, the false truths of nihilism and fundamentalism promulgate distorted world views and prevent true peace from taking root in a person's heart, one by denying the actual existence of truth itself, the other by imposing it.[20] The new evangelization talked about so much in recent years has desperate need of missionaries of the heart, those able to delve deep into the inner regions of the soul, to strike down the false ideologies that imprison the human spirit, and to relate to others on the level of their common humanity. There, in the depths of our hearts, we encounter the truth about ourselves and learn what it means to live at peace with ourselves, with God, and with one another.

Mass for the Election of a New Pope at St. Peter's Basilica on April, 18 2005.

[20] See Benedict XVI, *In Truth, Peace*, no. 10.

Since true peace of heart comes from God alone, we can prepare for it only by readying our hearts to receive it and to watch over it once it has arrived. We must remember, moreover, that peace of heart, even when authentic and true, can never be perfect in this life since it must resist temptation and can be lost through serious sin. For this reason, three important questions arise: (1) How do we acquire peace of heart? (2) What can we do to preserve peace of heart once we have it? (3) What can we do to get it back once we have lost it?

To respond to these questions, I would like to have recourse to some of the profound insights of *The Philokalia*, a work whose Greek title means, "love of the beautiful." My reason for doing so is to allow the great spiritual wealth of the Oriental churches to enter our discussion on truth and peace of heart, especially since the late-Pope John Paul II expressed his desire that Christ's Church on earth would learn to breathe once more with both of its lungs. The Eastern and Western expressions of the Christian faith, he believed, complemented one another and, when viewed together rather than in opposition to each other, would give rise to a fuller, more robust expression to the faith. Breathing with two lungs, he held, would be a great blessing for the Church and play an important role in the new evangelization of the Church in Europe and beyond.

In response to our first question, *The Philokalia* cites St. Gregory of Sinai (c. 1265-1346) that the energy of the Holy Spirit comes to us at baptism and can be unleashed in two ways: (1) through the fervent practice of the commandments and (2) through mindfulness of God that comes through spiritual guidance and by constantly calling upon the name of Jesus with conscious awareness.[21] In the first way, the energy of the Spirit reveals itself more slowly over time: "[T]o the degree to which we effectively practice the commandments its radiance is increasingly manifested in us."[22] This is another way of saying that we cannot separate our internal state from our actions in the world. Peace of heart manifests itself in right action and cannot exist apart from it. A reciprocal relationship exists between the two.

---

[21] *The Philokalia*, 4:259.

[22] Ibid.

Action flows from being—and vice versa. In the second way, the energy of the Spirit comes more quickly, if practiced properly and with proper direction. It affirms that, with God's help, we can develop a contemplative attitude toward life and become increasingly aware of God's presence within us and in all we do. Our mindfulness of God, one might say, relates closely to God's mindfulness of us. A skilled director can help us to narrow the gap between the two so that we may become ever more mindful of God's mindfulness of us. To this end, Gregory proposes the hesychast approach to prayer, which focuses on the continuous conscious (and eventual unconscious) invocation of the name of Jesus as a means arriving at a state of peace and inner stillness.

In response to our second question, *The Philokalia* says we preserve peace of heart through watchfulness and unceasing prayer. Watchfulness is a virtue closely associated with the search for stillness and purity of heart. It involves adopting an attitude of attentiveness over one's inner thoughts and feelings by maintaining guard over one's heart and intellect. Watchfulness is "spiritual sobriety, alertness, vigilance" and is opposed to "a state of drunken stupor."[23] One stays watchful over one's heart and intellect by trying to nurture inner stillness through unceasing prayer (1 Th 5:17). One can pray always by internalizing the words of the Jesus Prayer ("Lord Jesus Christ, Son of God, have mercy on me") so they penetrate and fully permeate one's mind and heart. This prayer is not a mere tool but an expression of living faith in Jesus Christ, the one true source of truth and life. Together, the goals of watchfulness and unceasing prayer are to keep a person in a state of dispassion and stillness so that God's Spirit might make its abode within the heart. Dispassion is a calming and transformation of the passions that puts one on fire with the love of God; stillness is a state of inner tranquility that gives a person a deep, abiding sense of God's presence. Because this inner tranquility or peace of heart is imperfect in this life and can even be lost, it is very important to ward off temptations and keep watch over it. If one lowers one's guard or ceases to pray,

---

[23] Ibid., 4:437.

one can be easily deceived and become easy prey for the destructive forces of the evil one.[24]

To respond to our third question, if one does happen to lose "peace of heart" through serious sin, *The Philokalia* says it can be regained through repentance and by shedding tears of compunction. As Nikitas Stithatos, the disciple and biographer of St. Symeon the New Theologian (949-1022), affirms: "...once the soul engages fervently and strenuously in the labors of repentance and we shed tears of compunction, then the prison-house is razed to the ground, the fire of the passions is extinguished, we are spiritually reborn through the abiding presence of the Paraclete, and once again the soul becomes a palace of purity and virginity."[25] Peace of heart, in other words, can be regained only if we express sincere and heartfelt sorrow for our sins. Once we do that, then God reenters the soul and imparts to it a threefold peace: (1) one which calms the hostile passions, (2) one which enables us to act according to our true nature, and (3) one which transforms us by

---

[24] Ibid., 4:429, 434-35, 437.

[25] Ibid., 4:120-21.

perfecting us into what is even beyond our nature.[26] This threefold peace reminds us that God wishes not merely to heal us, but also to enable us to be our truest selves, and even to transcend ourselves. He wishes us to become divinized, to share in his own nature, to be his adopted sons and daughters. When seen in this light, the education or formation of a person of peace requires that one recognize the truth about oneself before God and others. It means that one must recognize one's inner poverty and need for God and be willing to open one's heart to the rule and presence of God in one's life.

The Task of Peacemaking

"Peace," according to Archbishop Celestino Migliore, "implies a truth which is common to all peoples beyond cultural, philosophical, and religious diversities."[27] He goes on to root authentic

---

[26] Ibid., 4:121.

[27] Celestino Migliore, *Address to the U.N. General Assembly*, Friday, November 3, 2006. Reported on the Zenit website on November 7, 2006 as "Vatican: Dig-

peace in "the idea of the dignity of every human person intimately linked to the transcendent."[28] For Christians, this basic human truth flows from the belief that the human person is created in the image and likeness of God and that, through Christ, he or she can live in communion with the divine. If this is true, then one cannot be a person of peace if one has not first made peace with oneself and with God. That means allowing God to touch one's heart, transform it, and dwell within it. "A true peacemaker," according to Thomas Keating, the Trappist monk, spiritual writer, and well-known advocate of centering prayer, "is one who is willing to give up all myths of peace in order to receive 'the peace that the world cannot give.' He or she is one who has accepted Jesus' idea of the Kingdom, which is the knowledge and experience of the God of all creation as Abba— Jesus' endearing name for God the Father."[29]

---

nity of Person Is Basis for Peace." See, http://zenit.org/english.

[28] Ibid.

[29] Thomas Keating, "Peacemaking," *Contemplative Outreach Newsletter* 17(no. 2, Fall 2003/Winter 2004).

Peace, from this perspective, must first be found within oneself and flow outward from there. Only then will it be a true and authentic peace, only then will bring about a transformation of the world around us.

Robert M. Pirsig, the well-known (albeit controversial) American novelist and philosopher, is very much on target when he says: "Peace of mind produces right values, right values produce right thoughts. Right thoughts produce right actions and right actions produce work which will be a material reflection for others to see of the serenity at the center of it all." "Programs of a political nature," he goes on, "are important *end products* of social quality that can be effective only if the underlying structure of social values is right. The social values are right only if the individual values are right. The place to improve the world is first in one's own heart and head and hands, and then to work outward from there."[30] Similar ideas are re-

---

Available on the Contemplative Outreach website at: http://www.centeringprayer. com.

[30] Robert M. Pirsig, *Zen and the Art of Motorcycle Maintenance* (Toronto: Bantam Books, 1974), 267.

flected in a recent description of the Franciscan approach to peacemaking: "...he [Francis] believed peace cannot really be 'made.' Rather, it must be 'embodied'— personal spirituality must precede political reality. Peace for Franciscans is not an abstract ideal, nor is it a concept (such as Kant's notion of 'perpetual peace'), but it is *embodied* in individuals before it is *demonstrated* in communities."[31] Similar sentiments are reflected in the *Catechism of the Catholic Church*:

> It is necessary... to appeal to the spiritual and moral capacities of the human person and to the permanent need for his inner conversion, so as to obtain social changes that will really serve him. The *acknowledged priority of the conversion of heart* in no way eliminates but on the contrary imposes the obligation of bringing the appropriate remedies to institutions and living conditions when they are an inducement to sin, so that they conform to the

---

[31] Scott M. Thomas, "Franciscan Guide to Dialogue, *The Tablet* (October 7, 2006): 8.

norms of justice and advance the good rather than hinder it (italics mine).[32]

Benedict XVI once described "Peace" as "a task demanding of everyone a personal response consistent with God's plan." "The criterion inspiring this response" he maintains, "can only be *respect for the 'grammar' written on human hearts by the divine Creator*."[33] Elsewhere, he describes "Peace" as "the goal toward which all humanity aspires" and as "one of the most beautiful names of God."[34] He calls upon Catholics everywhere "to proclaim and *embody* ever more fully the 'Gospel of Peace'"(italics mine).[35] In his opinion, "[t]he great success of technology and science, which have notably improved humanity's conditions of life, do not give solutions to the most profound

---

[32] *Catechism of the Catholic Church*, par. 1888 (p. 461).

[33] Benedict XVI, *The Human Person, The Heart of Peace*, Message for the Celebration of the World Day of Peace, January 1, 2007, no. 3.

[34] Benedict XVI, *Homily for Vespers, First Sunday of Advent*, Saturday, December 2, 2006.

[35] Benedict XVI, *In Truth, Peace*, no. 11.

questions of the human spirit." "Only by openness to the mystery of God, who is love," he goes on, "can our hearts' thirst for truth and happiness be satisfied; only the perspective of eternity can give authentic value to historical events and above all to the mystery of human frailty, suffering and death."[36] Although peace must be promoted on every level and with every means possible in a broken world so prone to violence, Catholic teaching clearly acknowledges the importance and even the priority of "conversion of heart" as the most efficacious way people can be educated for peace.

Conclusion

What can we say by way of conclusion? Truth is one. What is true for the world and human society is also true for the human heart. To change the world for the better, we must first make a priority of changing the human heart. We can make strong inroads into changing the world by allow-

---

[36] Benedict XVI, *General Audience*, Wednesday, August 16, 2006.

ing God to touch our hearts and make his abode there. "The paradise of God," St. Alphonsus Maria de Liguori reminds us, "is the heart of man."[37] Peace comes to the world whenever God enters and dwells within our hearts. That is what we long for, and that is what God so earnestly desires. Jesus, the Prince of Peace and peacemaker par excellence, has come to the world to calm the anxieties of our hearts and offer us his peace. He offers us a true peace, an authentic peace, a peace the world cannot give.

The Blessings of the Beatitudes

- What is peace?
- Do you agree that it has to do with the tranquility of order?
- Do you agree that the lack of tranquility and order in society is a function of a lack of order and tranquility in our souls?

---

[37] Alphonsus de Liguori, *The Way to Converse Always and Familiarly with God* in *The Complete Work of St. Alphonsus Liguori*, 2:395.

- Do you know anyone that qualifies as a peacemaker?
- Does he or she possess a tranquil soul?
- Do you?

Prayer

Lord, I long for peace of mind, of heart, and in the world around me? Why is it that peace is so elusive, so difficult to achieve? Why is it that the peacemakers in our midst are rarely listened to, often persecuted, and even put to death? You are the Prince of Peace, and your Spirit gives us a peace the world cannot give. Help me to be open to your Spirit so that I might live in communion with you, experience the inner peace of your divine life, and share it with others in the hope of bringing peace to this weak and battered world.

Conclusion

The Eighth Beatitude

"Blessed are they who are persecuted for the sake of righteousness' sake, for theirs is the kingdom of heaven. Blessed are you when people revile you and persecute you and utter all kinds of evil against you falsely on my account. Rejoice and be glad, for your reward is great in heaven, for in the same way they persecuted the prophets who were before you" (Mt 5:10-12). According to Augustine, the eighth beatitude summarizes all the others and presents martyrdom as the ultimate expression of Christian discipleship.[1] When taken together, the beatitudes represent the attitudes of the kingdom, all of which find their deepest expression in the person of Jesus himself. To embody the beatitudes in our lives is another way of talking about the imitation of Christ. As the Apostle Paul reminds us in his letter to the Galatians, "I

---

[1] See Augustine of Hippo, *On the Sermon on the Mount*, Bk I, chap. 3; Pinckaers, *The Spirituality of Martyrdom*, 24.

have been crucified with Christ; and it is no longer I who live, but it is Christ who lives in me. And the life I now live in the flesh I live by faith in the Son of God, who loved me and gave himself for me" (Gal 2:19-20). The beatitudes represent the attitudes of the "friends of God," as the saints were known in the early Church, those followers so closely bound in friendship with Jesus that they experienced him living in and through them. So deep was this friendship that they lived as he lived and were willing to sacrifice everything for his sake, even their very lives!

The beatitudes have perennial significance not merely for the beauty of their words, but because they touch the very heart of the Jesus' Gospel message. They have great significance for us today because, as a society, we are in dire need of people who embrace them and through them seek to transform the world around them one heart at a time. "No slave can serve two masters; for a slave will either hate one and love the other, or be devoted to one a despise the other. You cannot serve God and wealth" (Lk 16:13). We live in a consumer and an entertainment culture.[2] We love our creature comforts, sometimes to such an extreme that we define our lives by them. I once read a religious caption that challenged us to take a good, hard look at the values by which we live. It read, "If you were on trial for being a Christian, would there be enough evidence to convict you?" The beatitudes remind us of the values that should take hold in our hearts and govern our lives. They are those embodied by Jesus himself and led him to make the ultimate sacrifice of giving his life for the world's salvation. The world (and Western society, in particular) has been described as *postmodern*, *secular*, and *liberal*. It is *postmodern* in that it has lost its faith in the power of reason, *secular* in that it has lost it sense of the sacred, *liberal* (in the classical sense of the term) in that it has exulted individual autonomy to the extreme.[3]

---

[2] Wayne Teasdale, *The Mystic Heart: Discovering a Universal Spirituality in the World's Religions* (Novato, CA: New World Library, 2001), 95.

[3] Nicanor Pier Giorgio Austriaco, *Biomedicine and Beatitude: An Introduction to Catholic Bioethics* (Washington, D. C.: The Catholic University of America Press, 2011), 5.

Now, perhaps more than ever, the world needs the values ("blessings") expressed in the beatitudes to help it find its bearings, navigate the turbulent waters of history, and make its way to its eternal destiny on distant shores revealed to us by the man from Galilee.